Bloom's Modern Critical Interpretations

Bloom's Modern Critical Interpretations

Stephen Crane's
The Red Badge of Courage
New Edition

Edited and with an introduction by
Harold Bloom
Sterling Professor of the Humanities
Yale University

**BLOOM'S
LITERARY CRITICISM**
An imprint of Infobase Publishing

Bloom's Modern Critical Interpretations: The Red Badge of Courage—New Edition

Copyright © 2010 by Infobase Publishing
Introduction © 2010 by Harold Bloom

Bloom's Literary Criticism
An imprint of Infobase Publishing
132 West 31st Street
New York NY 10001

Library of Congress Cataloging-in-Publication Data
Stephen Crane's The red badge of courage / edited and with an introduction by Harold Bloom. — New ed.
    p. cm. — (Bloom's modern critical interpretations)
  Includes bibliographical references and index.
  ISBN 978-1-60413-889-4 (hardcover)
  1. Crane, Stephen, 1871–1900. Red badge of courage.   2. United States—History—Civil War, 1861–1865—Literature and the war.   I. Bloom, Harold.   II. Title: Red badge of courage.
  PS1449.C85R397 2010
  813'.4—dc22
                                2010019263

Contributing editor: Pamela Loos
Cover design by Takeshi Takahashi
Composition by IBT Global, Troy NY
Cover printed by IBT Global, Troy NY
Book printed and bound by IBT Global, Troy NY
Date printed: September 2010
Printed in the United States of America

10 9 8 7 6 5 4 3 2 1

Contents

Editor's Note

My introduction broods on Stephen Crane's impressionistic mode and on its aptness for representing battle.

Harold Beaver's classic essay defines the ethos of heroism in Crane as "nervous integrity," an apt term for Joseph Conrad before Crane and Ernest Hemingway after him.

Mary Neff Shaw interprets *Red Badge* as a satiric novel, while Philip D. Beidler finds Henry Fleming as alternating "momentary cowardice" and "momentary valor."

Hints of Henry's attraction to an archetypal dark woman are explored by Verner D. Mitchell, after which Max Westbrook asserts that in Crane's cosmos both cynicism and idealism are shown to distort reality.

Benjamin F. Fisher summarizes the contemporary British reactions to *Red Badge*, while Andrew Lawson looks at concealed class conflict in the novel.

Courage and its ambiguities are the theme of Michael Schaefer, after which Perry Lentz teases out some of the implications of Crane's prose style.

In this volume's well-informed final essay, Roy Morris Jr. traces *Red Badge*'s ancestry in Tolstoy, Ambrose Bierce, and others.

HAROLD BLOOM

Introduction

Stephen Crane's contribution to the canon of American literature is fairly slight in bulk: one classic short novel, three vivid stories, and two or three ironic lyrics. *The Red Badge of Courage*; "The Open Boat," "The Blue Hotel," and "The Bride Comes to Yellow Sky"; "War Is Kind" and "A Man Adrift on a Slim Spar"—a single small volume can hold them all. Crane was dead at 28, after a frantic life, but a longer existence probably would not have enhanced his achievement. He was an exemplary American writer, flaring in the forehead of the morning sky and vanishing in the high noon of our evening land. An original, if not quite a great original, he prophesied Hemingway and our other journalist-novelists and still seems a forerunner of much to come.

The Red Badge of Courage is Crane's undoubted masterwork. Each time I reread it, I am surprised afresh, particularly by the book's originality, which requires a reader's act of recovery because Crane's novel has been so influential. To write about battle in English, since Crane, is to be shadowed by Crane. Yet Crane, who later saw warfare in Cuba and between the Greeks and the Turks in his work as a correspondent, had experienced no fighting when he wrote *The Red Badge of Courage*. There is no actual experience that informs Crane's version of the battle of Chancellorsville, one of the most terrible carnages of the American Civil War. Yet anyone who has gone through warfare, from the time of the novel's publication (1895) until now, has testified to Crane's uncanny accuracy at the representation of battle. *The Red Badge of Courage* is an impressionist's triumph, in the particular sense that "impressionist" had in the literature of the nineties, a Paterian sense that went back to the emphasis on seeing in Carlyle, Emerson, and Ruskin. Conrad and Henry James, both of whom befriended Crane, had

1

their own relation to the impressionist mode, and each realized that Crane was a pure or natural impressionist, indeed the only one, according to Conrad.

Pater, deftly countering Matthew Arnold, stated the credo of literary impressionism:

> The first step towards seeing one's object as it really is, is to know one's impression as it really is, to discriminate it, to realize it distinctly.

Pater's "object" is a work of art, verbal or visual, but the critic here has stated Stephen Crane's quest to see the object of experience as it is, to know one's impression of it, and to realize that impression in narrative fiction. Scholarly arguments as to whether and to what degree *The Red Badge of Courage* is naturalistic, symbolist, or impressionist can be set aside quickly. Joyce's *Ulysses* is both naturalistic and symbolist within the general perspective of the Paterian or impressionistic "epiphany" or privileged moment, but juxtapose *Red Badge* to *Ulysses* and Crane is scarcely naturalistic or symbolist in comparison. Crane is altogether an impressionist, in his "vivid impressionistic description of action on that woodland battlefield," as Conrad phrased it, or, again in Conrad's wording, in "the imaginative analysis of his own temperament tried by the emotions of a battlefield."

If Crane's impressionism had a single literary origin, as to some extent is almost inevitable, Kipling is that likely forerunner. The puzzles of literary ancestry are most ironical here, since Kipling's precursor was Mark Twain. Hemingway's famous observation that all modern American literature comes out of one book, *Adventures of Huckleberry Finn*, is only true of Crane, the indubitable beginning of our modern literature, insofar as Crane took from Kipling precisely what the author of *The Light That Failed* and *Kim* owed to Twain. Michael Fried's association of Crane with the painter Thomas Eakins is peculiarly persuasive, since Crane's visual impressionism is so oddly American, without much resembling Whistler's. Crane is almost the archetype of the writer as a child of experience, yet I think this tends to mean that then there are a few strong artistic precursors, rather than a tradition that makes itself available. Associate Crane with Kipling and Eakins on the way to, but still a distance from, Conrad and the French postimpressionists, and you probably have stationed him accurately enough.

The Red Badge of Courage is necessarily a story about fear. Crane's Young Soldier, again as Conrad noted, "dreads not danger but fear itself. . . . In this he stands for the symbol of all untried men." Henry Fleming, as eventually we come to know the Young Soldier, moves ironically from a dangerous self-doubt to what may be an even more dangerous dignity. This is the novel's famous yet perhaps equivocal conclusion:

For a time this pursuing recollection of the tattered man took all elation from the youth's veins. He saw his vivid error, and he was afraid that it would stand before him all his life. He took no share in the chatter of his comrades, nor did he look at them or know them, save when he felt sudden suspicion that they were seeing his thoughts and scrutinizing each detail of the scene with the tattered soldier.

Yet gradually he mustered force to put the sin at a distance. And at last his eyes seemed to open to some new ways. He found that he could look back upon the brass and bombast of his earlier gospels and see them truly. He was gleeful when he discovered that he now despised them.

With this conviction came a store of assurance. He felt a quiet manhood, nonassertive but of sturdy and strong blood. He knew that he would no more quail before his guides wherever they should point. He had been to touch the great death, and found that, after all, it was but the great death. He was a man.

So it came to pass that as he trudged from the place of blood and wrath his soul changed. He came from hot plowshares to prospects of clover tranquilly, and it was as if hot plowshares were not. Scars faded as flowers.

It rained. The procession of weary soldiers became a bedraggled train, despondent and muttering, marching with churning effort in a trough of liquid brown mud under a low, wretched sky. Yet the youth smiled, for he saw that the world was a world for him, though many discovered it to be made of oaths and walking sticks. He had rid himself of the red sickness of battle. The sultry nightmare was in the past. He had been an animal blistered and sweating in the heat and pain of war. He turned now with a lover's thirst to images of tranquil skies, fresh meadows, cool brooks—an existence of soft and eternal peace.

Over the river a golden ray of sun came through the hosts of leaden rain clouds.

More Hemingway than Hemingway are these very American sentences: "He had been to touch the great death, and found that, after all, it was but the great death. He was a man." Is the irony of that dialectical enough to suffice? In context, the power of the irony is beyond question, since Crane's prose is strong enough to bear rephrasing as: "He had been to touch the great fear, and found that, after all, it was still the great fear. He was not yet a man." Crane's saving nuance is that the fear of being afraid dehumanizes, while accepting one's own mortality bestows on one the association with others that grants the dignity of the human. How does Crane's prose find the strength to sustain a vision that primary and normative? The answer, I suspect, is the Bible and Bunyan, both of them deeply at work in this unbelieving son of a Methodist minister: "He came from hot plowshares to prospects of clover tranquilly, and it was as if hot plowshares were not." The great trope of Isaiah is assimilated in the homely and unassuming manner of Bunyan, and we see the Young Soldier, Henry Fleming, as an American pilgrim, anticipating when both sides of the Civil War "shall beat their swords into plowshares, and their spears into pruning hooks."

Crane's accurate apprehension of the phantasmagoria that is battle has been compared to Tolstoy's. There is something to such a parallel, perhaps because Tolstoy even more massively is a biblical writer. What is uniquely Crane's, what parts him from all prior visionaries of warfare, is difficult to define but is of the highest importance for establishing his astonishing originality. Many examples might be chosen, but I give the death of the color sergeant from the conclusion of chapter 19:

> Over the field went the scurrying mass. It was a handful of men splattered into the faces of the enemy. Toward it instantly sprang the yellow tongues. A vast quantity of blue smoke hung before them. A nighty banging made ears valueless.
>
> The youth ran like a madman to reach the woods before a bullet could discover him. He ducked his head low, like a football player. In his haste his eyes almost closed, and the scene was a wild blur. Pulsating saliva stood at the corners of his mouth.
>
> Within him, as he hurled himself forward, was born a love, a despairing fondness for this flag which was near him. It was a creation of beauty and invulnerability. It was a goddess, radiant, that bended its form with an imperious gesture to him. It was a woman, red and white, hating and loving, that called him with the voice of his hopes. Because no harm could come to it he endowed it with power. He kept near, as if it could be a saver of lives, and an imploring cry went from his mind.
>
> In the mad scramble he was aware that the color sergeant flinched suddenly, as if struck by a bludgeon. He faltered, and then became motionless, save for his quivering knees.
>
> He made a spring and a clutch at the pole. At the same instant his friend grabbed it from the other side. They jerked at it, stout and furious, but the color sergeant was dead, and the corpse

would not relinquish its trust. For a moment there was a grim encounter. The dead man, swinging with bended back, seemed to be obstinately tugging, in ludicrous and awful ways, for the possession of the flag.

It was past in an instant of time. They wrenched the flag furiously from the dead man, and, as they turned again, the corpse swayed forward with bowed head. One arm swung high, and the curved hand fell with heavy protest on the friend's unheeding shoulder.

In the "wild blur" of this phantasmagoria, there are two images of pathos, the flag and the corpse of the color sergeant. Are they not to some degree assimilated to each other, so that the corpse becomes a flagpole and the flag a corpse? Yet so dialectical is the interplay of Crane's biblical irony that the assimilation, however incomplete, itself constitutes a figure of doubt as to the normative intensities of patriotism and group solidarity that the scene exemplifies, both in the consciousness of Henry Fleming and in that of the rapt reader. The "despairing fondness" for the flag is both a Platonic and a Freudian eros but finally more Freudian. It possesses "invulnerability" for which the soldier under fire has that Platonic desire for what he himself does not possess and quite desperately needs, but it manifests even more a Freudian sense of the ambivalence both of and toward the woman as object of the drive, at once a radiant goddess sexually bending her form though imperiously, yet also a woman, red and white, hating and loving, destroying and healing.

The corpse of the color sergeant, an emblem of devotion to the flag and the group even beyond death, nevertheless keeps Fleming and his friend from the possibility of survival as men, compelling them to clutch and jerk at the pole, stout and furious. Life-in-death incarnate, the corpse obstinately tugs for the staff of its lost life. Homer surely would have appreciated the extraordinary closing gesture, as the corpse sways forward, head bowed but arm swung high for a final stroke, as "the curved hand fell with heavy protest on the friend's unheeding shoulder."

Crane is hardly the American Homer; Walt Whitman occupies that place forever. Still, *The Red Badge of Courage* is certainly the most Homeric prose narrative ever written by an American. One wants to salute it with Whitman's most Homeric trope, when he says of the grass:

And now it seems to me the beautiful uncut hair of graves.

HAROLD BEAVER

Stephen Crane: The Hero as Victim

We picture the world as thick with conquering and elate humanity,
but here, with the bugles of the tempest pealing, it was hard to
imagine a peopled earth. One viewed the existence of man then
as a marvel, and conceded a glamor of wonder to these lice, which
were caused to cling to a whirling, fire-smote, ice-locked, disease-
stricken, space-lost bulb. The conceit of man was explained by this
storm to be the very engine of life. (*The Blue Hotel*, Chapter 8)

By the late nineteenth century the heroic ideal, though noisily encouraged
in romantic fiction and by the popular press, had become harder and harder to
sustain. For the myth of heroism was dependent on free will. But what Men-
del and Ricardo and Marx and Darwin and Freud and Malthus had seemingly
taught was that man was trapped; that he was the unsuspecting victim of
genetic and economic and political and evolutionary and psychological forces,
including an ever-spiralling population growth. The myth of heroism, moreover, depended on a vision of an integrated society with its own economic and
sexual hierarchies, its own natural and supernatural controls. But, by the end
of the century, the whole universe, it seemed, had disintegrated into a chaos
of competing and anarchic forces, receding ever faster to a state of entropic
collapse. Such forces, by definition, were beyond human control. No counter-
attack, however defiant, could be waged by an individual alone.

From *The Yearbook of English Studies* 12, Heroes and the Heroic Special Number (1982):
186–93. Copyright © 1982 by the Modern Humanities Research Association.

By collective action, perhaps: 'The mode of production of material life', Marx had written in his preface to *The Critique of Political Economy*, 'conditions the general process of social, political and intellectual life'. Or, as the American Henry George put it, 'the idea that man mentally and physically is the result of slow modifications, perpetuated by heredity, irresistibly suggests the idea that it is the race life, not the individual life, which is the object of human existence'.[1] Such was the gospel of *Progress and Poverty* (1879). But the authorship of books was hardly ever collective; it was indifferent to progress; and by the late nineteenth century had become even more inturned, if anything, to individual 'human existence'. The overriding task remained, as always, one of composition. That alone, in a decomposing universe, made the writer's role potentially heroic.

Stephen Crane was among the most self-conscious of this new breed of heroic writers. Henry Adams, his fellow American, chose to confront the *intellectual* responsibility of opting for anarchy.[2] Crane chose to confront the *moral* responsibility (amid 'the bugles of the tempest pealing') of reeling through the blizzard. For it was as if a blizzard had struck the old American certainties. The new forces of Hegelian idealism and Darwinian biology and economic determinism—of evolution, class warfare, and heredity—were peculiarly stacked against the old Jeffersonian belief in personal self-control. Romantic individualism quickly soured, in the decades after the Civil War, to a documentary pessimism. Even before 1860 a brilliant minority of American writers, which included Hawthorne and Melville, had opted for pessimism. But now there were mass deserters. By 1900 the cleft between high art and 'pop' art was complete. It opened a chasm between serious fiction and fun, or escapist uplift, in westerns and athletic 'profiles' of which we are the inevitable heirs. For it was in this generation that the moral rewards of capitalism were first subverted; that Horatio Alger's call of 'rags to riches', 'Log Cabin to White House', was finally undercut by the new Naturalist Novel. The hero of self-improvement, U.S.-style, was shown, for good or ill, to be a mere victim of circumstances and/or his own illusions.

One native response was to ask: 'So what?' 'What, in short', in the words of William James, 'is the truth's cash value in experiential terms?'.[3] But pragmatism was of little use to men who felt already doomed; for whom both Christianity and the promise of the Greek Revival had failed; who felt excluded from both the old religious and the Homeric appeals to personal glory. Like Dante, the young Stephen Crane awoke to find all confused, all lost. 'He had long despaired of witnessing a Greeklike struggle.'[4] He aimed to fight his way out of that modern *selva oscura*, or Darwinian jungle. *The Red Badge of Courage* was to be his report from the jungle.

It appeared in 1895, a year after Kipling's *The Jungle Book*, four years before Conrad's *Heart of Darkness*. Crane was still only twenty-four years old. His subject was that of the hunters and the hunted, of the predators and the victims (much as that of Joel Chandler Harris's *Uncle Remus* tales) in a savagely destructive world. But his literary talent lay far from vernacular or folk tale. It comprised, above all, a split-second marksmanship in stalking his prey, nicknamed by contemporary photojournalists the 'snapshot'. This new heroic style was to rival Homer's for clarity. This new American *Iliad*, too, was subdivided into twenty-four parts. Had not the war, which it commemorated, been won by Ulysses S. Grant? Had not the artist, who first commemorated it, himself been called Winslow Homer? Like that American Homer's, Crane's theme was to be read as neither the romance of heroism, nor the triumph of heroism, but the quandary of heroism in an unheroic age, or rather (to use the title of one of his own later stories) the 'Mystery of Heroism'.

For the Darwinian metaphor, red in tooth and claw, had been miraculously turned inside out on that battlefield to become a scenario for this 'naturalist', or reportage-like, fiction. Here Crane could study the human condition, in all its turbulence, with the most exacting details of historical research. In this, too, he proved himself to be profoundly American. However realistic his setting, or his tone, he was still writing 'romances', like his great contemporary, Henry James. What Puritan New England had been for Hawthorne, the Virginian landscape of the Civil War was to be for Crane. Instead of the meeting-houses and custom-houses, the colonial wilderness and the Indians of the North, he would present the pine barrens, in mist and gunsmoke, of the South. Instead of a *Scarlet Letter*, he would depict a *Red Badge* of shame. Only the meaning shifts. Hawthorne's 'letters of guilt' would here turn to 'red letters of curious revenge'. For the theme was no longer that of lust, or some Faustian perusal of sin on a black-and-white frontier, but the psychological backlash of fear.

Just as Hawthorne, furthermore, had studied John Mason and William Hubbard and Cotton and Increase Mather (his seventeenth-century sources for the Indian Wars), so Crane pored over the *Battles and Leaders of the Civil War*,[5] Harper's *History*, the drawings of Winslow Homer, and the photographs of Mathew Brady. Their battle scenes became for him a kind of ritual test, a crisis of identity even. He had missed the Great War. He belonged to a post-war generation, guiltily hankering for some extreme engagement in a commercial and prosaic age. He studied the plans of the attacks and counter-attacks of the battle of Chancellorsville (2–4 May 1863). He mentally reconstructed that wilderness, ten miles west of Fredericksburg on the Rappahannock River, in which Sedgwick and Hooker were forced back across the river by Lee's bluff, and the brilliant fifteen-mile flanking attack, in which Stonewall Jackson was mortally wounded. This was Lee's last great victory, leading to his invasion of the North in the Gettysburg Campaign. It becomes the visual and tactical source for *The Red Badge of Courage*.

For the fictional exercise came first. The emotional rehearsal came first. As with many young writers, Crane's career seems curiously inverted, though what began as a purely literary experience eventually took him to Mexico, and to Cuba and Greece to cover the Turkish War as a war correspondent. Later, when he came to write *The Open Boat*, his text recreated the context of his own life. But when he wrote *The Red Badge of Courage* his text had to follow another's text. It was from Stendhal's *Le Rouge et le Noir*, from Tolstoy's *Sevastopol Sketches* and the great Borodino scenes, as viewed by Pierre in *War and Peace*, that Crane learnt to use his single incoherent angle of vision. For the confusion of soldiers and cavalry charges, the roar of guns and crackle of rifles, the whole mad inconsequence of war were for Crane hugely symbolic of all terror, all uncertainty, all ultimate loneliness. Everything is questioned: the battle, the wound, the heroism, the resolution and self-respect reassembled out of doubts and lies. Crane's Chancellorsville is revealed as a cosmic trap, an absurd non-event. In the final chapter, the regiment finds itself winding back to the river it had originally crossed a few days earlier, as if nothing had happened.

For nothing, in a sense, had happened. Nothing ever happens. Everything becomes part of the antics of non-communication, which was to become Crane's final symbol (in *The Open Boat*) for the existential void in which his actors prate and strut and cower and flee; and sometimes survive; and sometimes face death with a steady dignity and calm. Battle lust is directly compared to a mad religion; the Civil War, to a sectarian conflict—as if fought by lapsed Methodists to the tune of:

> Fight the good fight with all thy might,
> Christ is thy strength, and Christ thy right;
> Lay hold on life, and it shall be
> Thy joy and crown eternally ...
>
> Faint not nor fear. His arms are near,
> He changeth not, and thou art dear;
> Only believe, and thou shalt see
> That Christ is all in all to thee.[6]

'Well, God reigns, and in his hands we are safe, whatever awaits us', was his father's habitual refrain. Again and again (in *Maggie*, in *George's Mother*, in *The Blue Hotel*, in *The Bride Comes to Yellow Sky*) Stephen Crane seems to confront his father's snug Methodism, while simultaneously questioning the American demand for aggression, the American pride in the predatory tough guy, the Bowery kid with patent-leather shoes 'like weapons',[7] or Westerners with guns on their hips. The attack is two-pronged.

For *The Red Badge of Courage* is charged with religious imagery: the *Ecce Homo* of the 'dead man who was seated with his back against a columnlike tree'; the notorious red sun 'pasted in the sky like a wafer'. Yet the communion of modern warfare proves a camaraderie of the absurd. The sacrifice of Jim Conklin (another J.C.) turns to a pointless *danse-macabre*, like the 'devotee of a mad religion, blood-sucking, muscle-wrenching, bone-crushing'. The red badge of courage itself proves to be panic-stricken and self-inflicted. Self-discovery and personal salvation turn out inevitably to be a patched lie in a meaningless war. Even to bear the colours, that sacred trust, is merely to feel 'the daring spirit of a savage religion-mad'.[8] All attempts to shape a moral vision are ultimately reduced to madness in an amoral universe. For 'secular and religious education had' by no means 'effaced the throat-grappling instinct', nor 'firm finance held in check the passions'.[9] From Crane's desperate vision runs a direct line to Hemingway's nihilist litanies.

H. G. Wells was right when he wrote that Crane's writings suggested not so much Tolstoy, or Conrad's *Lord Jim*, as Whistler. Wells praised him for his 'impressionism'.[10] We might prefer to use 'expressionism' for those suns and wounds entangled in a single obsession, like Van Gogh's *Sunflowers*, or Edvard Munch's *The Scream*. Brown, red, yellow, blue, grey, green, are laid on with a pointillist discretion, learnt from the emotive spectrum of Goethe's *Colour Lore*. Even in his titles: *The Red Badge of Courage*; *The Black Riders*; *The Blue Hotel*; *The Bride Comes to Yellow Sky*. His snapshot vision has the terrible, often hallucinatory, clarity of dream:

> Once he found himself almost into a swamp. He was obliged to walk upon bog tufts and watch his feet to keep from the oily mire. Pausing at one time to look about him he saw, out at some black water, a small animal pounce in and emerge directly with a gleaming fish.
>
> The youth went again into the deep thickets. The brushed branches made a noise that drowned the sounds of cannon. He walked on, going from obscurity into promises of a greater obscurity.
>
> At length he reached a place where the high, arching boughs made a chapel. He softly pushed the green doors aside and entered. Pine needles were a gentle brown carpet. There was a religious half light.

Near the threshold he stopped, horror-stricken at the sight of a thing.

He was being looked at by a dead man who was seated with his back against a columnlike tree. The corpse was dressed in a uniform that once had been blue, but was now faded to a melancholy shade of green. The eyes, staring at the youth, had changed to the dull hue to be seen on the side of a dead fish. The mouth was open. Its red had changed to an appalling yellow. Over the gray skin of the face ran little ants. One was trundling some sort of a bundle along the upper lip. (*The Red Badge of Courage*, Chapter 7)

Concentrate. Focus. Advance. After the 'pounce', a 'trundling': and the 'gleaming fish' reemerges a 'dead fish', while those primary reds and blues are dissolved, in alliteration, to a foggy yellow and pervasive green.

Such shifts of mood and their ironies constitute the pattern of Crane's work. Though capable of explication, like the symbolism of Van Gogh's canvases, they ultimately resist—must resist—a reductive interpretation into patterns of moral and spiritual significance. In this Crane is not like Hawthorne, nor fundamentally, I think, like Melville. Henry Fleming ('the youth' of *The Red Badge of Courage*) can never be wholly educated out of his illusions, his fantasies, his flickering shifts of mood. Crane did his best to impose an ending:

Yet gradually he mustered force to put the sin at a distance. And at last his eyes seemed to open to some new ways. He found that he could look back upon the brass and bombast of his earlier gospels and see them truly. He was gleeful when he discovered that he now despised them.

With the conviction came a store of assurance. He felt a quiet manhood, nonassertive but of sturdy and strong blood. He knew that he would no more quail before his guides wherever they should point. He had been to touch the great death, and found that, after all, it was but the great death. He was a man. (*The Red Badge of Courage*, Chapter 24)

But that seems rather pretentious, strained. He tried rewriting it several times. For just as Henry had fled from battle, in pursuit of a squirrel skittering into the trees, so the blind rage that turns him into a hero, a flag-bearer in the end, is mere animal rage. Man is out of control: that is the burden of Crane's message. Far from reason or courage, it is illusion and impulse, again and again, that twitches and throws us.

The Red Badge of Courage reads like some zany inscrutable allegory of *non-sense*. Crane's soldiers are seldom named: 'the youth' (Henry Fleming), the 'tall soldier' (Jim Conklin), the 'loud soldier' (Wilson), the 'spectral soldier', the 'tattered man', the man with a 'cheery voice', the man with a shoeful of blood who 'hopped like a schoolboy in a game', who 'was laughing hysterically'. A decade earlier, in *Specimen Days*, Whitman had written of the unknown dead, 'The Million Dead':

> (In some of the cemeteries nearly *all* the dead are unknown. At Salisbury, N.C., for instance, the known are only 85, while the unknown are 12,027, and 11,700 of these are buried in trenches. A national monument has been put up here, by order of Congress, to mark the spot—but what visible, material monument can ever fittingly commemorate that spot?)[11]

It was Crane who composed that 'visible, material monument'. Long before the multiplication of Tombs of Unknown Warriors throughout the world, Crane had revealed that warrior, with his schoolboy hop and hysterical laugh, as the scared and impotent victim. Long before Wilfred Owen and Siegfried Sassoon, Crane had confronted the chauvinism, the imperialism, the patriotic humbug of a bellicose decade that gloried in the honour and self-sacrifice of war. In modern wars, he taught, it is the victims who are greeted as heroes.

For death, he realized, *exposes* man. It is the final betrayal of lives mercifully protected by shame, concealment, lies. Like the paper-thin torn soles of the shoes on the feet of a fallen soldier: 'it was as if fate had betrayed the soldier. In death it exposed to his enemies that poverty which in life he had perhaps concealed from his friends'.[12] Wounds, however, may strangely glorify a man. As he declared in 'An Episode of War':

> A wound gives strange dignity to him who bears it. Well men shy from his new and terrible majesty. It is as if the wounded man's hand is upon the curtain which hangs before the revelations of all existence—the meaning of ants, potentates, wars, cities, sunshine, snow, a feather dropped from a bird's wing; and the power of it sheds radiance upon a bloody form, and makes the other men understand sometimes that they are little.[13]

Crane himself, throughout his short career, seems a wounded man, a suicidally haunted man, in his far-ranging quest for wars from Cuba to Turkey. At the time of writing *The Red Badge of Courage* he had come no closer to war than Philoctetes. Like Hemingway, his heir, he seems a ready-made case-book study for Edmund Wilson's *The Wound and the Bow*. All his fiction, whether set in the Bowery or in the Virginian or Western wilds, seems to fashion his own psychological skirmish, in tougher and tougher engagements, with the amoral, aggressive, commercial, bourgeois jungle of the 1890s.

How does one plot a meaningful life? How plot a meaningful life in such a meaningless universe? Man cannot be wholly predetermined, he seems to say. Economic and social and hereditary environment cannot be all. Men *must* be seen as first movers. Men *must* retain the illusion of free will, to operate in spite of their environment. Against the sins of pride and self-delusion, the sycophantic faith in society's codes and the dogmas of God, must be asserted the moral responsibility of self-definition. 'In a story of mine called "An Experiment in Misery"', he wrote, 'I tried to make plain that the root of Bowery life is a sort of cowardice. Perhaps I mean a lack of ambition or to willingly be knocked flat and accept the licking'.[14] Crane viewed the bums of the Bowery flophouses uncompromisingly. Cowards are those who cannot confront the question of self-definition. Heroes can and do. Cowards are those who fall prey to social delusions, from whom Crane abdicates all responsibility as a writer. Cowards are those who fail to stand up against the 'collaboration of sin', like the Easterner in tacit alliance with the card-sharper (of *The Blue Hotel*) versus an outsider. The iron bars of tradition and of the law in which man travels Crane called 'a moving box'.[15] The problem is that of living without bars, without order, outside dogmas or codes, in a blizzard of whirling and competing forces. The question is one of decomposition with dignity in a decomposing universe. Not only the roles but the writing must be disintegrated to reassert our inherent worth and dignity as men.

The ultimate question is that of heroism: not the passionate heroism of Crane's pseudo-heroes—rushing to save, to kill, to prop the flag—but the stoic restraint of a Jim Conklin (in *The Red Badge of Courage*) or the correspondent (in *The Open Boat*). Neither the Swede fuelled on Scully's whisky (in *The Blue Hotel*), nor black Henry Johnson rushing into a blazing laboratory (in *The Monster*), nor Fred Collins recklessly crossing noman's land for some water (in 'A Mystery of Heroism'), nor Henry Fleming in his final berserker fury, is a hero. All are 'blindly led by quaint emotions'.[16] All, even at best, are masters merely of their own visionary worlds. As Emily Dickinson once put it:

> A coward will remain, Sir,
>   Until the fight is done;
> But an *immortal hero*
>   Will take his hat, and run![17]

True heroes act with a nervous integrity: 'as deliberate and exact as so many watchmakers', as Crane wrote of the Cuban conflict.[18] In his final writings (in 'The Veteran', 'The Price of the Harness', *Wounds in the Rain*, the Spitzbergen tales) Crane dealt increasingly with such cool deliberation. Theirs is the dignity of self-possession. Heroes are those who can go forward, alone; who accept moral responsibility for themselves and others; who can accept isolation; who remain committed to life; who stand up to the 'collaboration of sin'. Though they too, of course, must die. They too, like Jim Conklin, may at any moment collapse with an animal-like kick of death.

Crane's heroes cradle their wounds in careful self-support, grabbing their left arm with their right hand, or holding their right wrist tenderly as if it were 'made of very brittle glass'. For Crane saw through the dignity to the fragility and the pathos of self-possession. He was still only twenty-eight years old when he died. It was of tuberculosis that he died. Within a generation his fragile dignity was reduced to a mere code, a moral shorthand for stoic self-definition and self-control. That is often called Hemingway's code.

Yet Hemingway also delivered Crane's finest epitaph. 'What about the good writers?', asks a German in *Green Hills of Africa*. 'The good writers are Henry James, Stephen Crane and Mark Twain', Hemingway replies. 'That's not the order they're good in. There is no order for good writers'. And what happened to Crane, the German asks. 'He died. That's simple. He was dying from the start.'[19]

Notes

1. *A Contribution to the Critique of Political Economy* (1859), translated by S. W. Ryazanskaya (Moscow, 1971); *Progress and Poverty* (New York, 1879), 'Conclusion'.

2. See *The Education of Henry Adams* (Washington, 1907), especially Chapters 33–34.

3. 'What Pragmatism Means', *Pragmatism: A New Name for Some Old Ways of Thinking* (New York, 1907), Chapter 2.

4. *The Red Badge of Courage* (New York, 1895), Chapter 1.

5. *Battles and Leaders of the Civil War; being for the most part contributions by Union and Confederate officers; based upon 'The Century War Series'*, edited by the editorial staff of *The Century Magazine*, 4 vols (New York, 1884–87).

6. John Samuel Bewley Monsell, 'Fight of Faith', *Hymns of Love and Praise for the Church's Year* (London, 1863).

7. *Maggie: A Girl of the Streets* (New York, 1893), Chapter 5.

8. Chapters 7, 9, 23.

9. This whole passage stands as a deliberately misleading signpost at the opening of *The Red Badge of Courage*: 'From his home his youthful eyes had looked upon the war in his own country with distrust. It must be some sort of a play affair. He had long despaired of witnessing a Greeklike struggle. Such would be no more, he had said. Men were better, or more timid. Secular and religious education had

effaced the throat-grappling instinct, or else firm finance held in check the passions' (Chapter 1). 'The Education of Henry Fleming', as it were, was precisely to learn that contemporary man (himself included) was neither better, nor more timid.

10. 'Stephen Crane from an English Standpoint', *North American Review*, 171 (August 1900), 233–42.

11. 'The Million Dead, Too, Summ'd Up', *Specimen Days & Collect* (Philadelphia, 1882).

12. *The Red Badge of Courage*, Chapter 3.

13. *Last Words* (London, 1902).

14. Crane writing to Catherine Harris on 12 November 1896: *Stephen Crane: Letters*, edited by R. W. Stallman and Lillian Gilkes (New York, 1960). p. 133.

15. *The Red Badge of Courage*, Chapter 3.

16. 'A Mystery of Heroism', *The Little Regiment* (New York, 1896).

17. Written in 1852: *The Poems of Emily Dickinson*, edited by Thomas H. Johnson (Cambridge, Massachusetts, 1955), Number 3.

18. *Wounds in the Rain* was a fictional adaptation of Crane's own adventures with the American forces in Cuba, 1898.

19. *Green Hills of Africa* (New York, 1935), Part 1, Chapter 1.

MARY NEFF SHAW

Henry Fleming's Heroics in The Red Badge of Courage: A Satiric Search for a "Kinder, Gentler" Heroism

In spite of the great body of critical work surrounding *The Red Badge of Courage*, eminent critics, as Edwin Cady, continue to call for a coherent and comprehensive study that "penetrate[s]" the "mystery" of Crane's works, which remain "elusive."[1] Similarly, Milne Holton identifies the persistent frustration of attempting to understand Crane's works: "The centers of Crane's stories remain obscure . . . Too often an understanding of one story, when finally arrived at, contradicts a seemingly sound assertion about another."[2] In their queries about *Red Badge* most critics ponder Henry Fleming's heroism, specifically whether the reader should accept Fleming's assertion that "he was now what he called a hero"[3] at face value or not. Unfortunately, scholars who accept the denotative meaning of Fleming's assertion cannot account for the incongruencies between Fleming's deduction and his actions, and scholars who conclude that the denotative meaning of *Red Badge* is not reliable generally rely on such techniques as irony or multiple viewpoints as their critical methodology. However, identifying the extent to which a smattering of truth may be present in a number of viewpoints is impossible, since multiple viewpoints, which lack consistent guidelines for evaluation, blur thematic intentions according to Joseph Brennan.[4] Or, as Donald Pizer observes, Crane's use of viewpoint in *Red Badge* creates "ambivalence" because we are "not always certain of an author's judgment

From *Studies in the Novel* 22, no. 4 (Winter 1990): 418–28. Copyright © 1990 by the University of North Texas.

of his character's action and value."[5] Equally elusive is the exclusive implementation of irony as critical cipher. As Steven Mailloux argues, "complete explicitness of irony is an impossibility," resulting in "ambiguity, the indecision between interpretation of irony and nonirony."[6] Mailloux then concludes that "ambiguity in *Red Badge* must be a function of an interpretation rather than of the text." However, Donald Pizer posits that the ambiguity in *Red Badge* is authorial.[7] Pizer's assessment is verified by Crane in one of his letters. Agreeing with Emerson, whom he quotes, Crane writes: "Preaching is fatal to art in literature . . . There should be a long logic beneath the story, but it should be kept carefully out of sight."[8]

If, as Crane acknowledges, the "logic" or "mystery" or "center" of the story should be hidden from obvious view, and if, as Mailloux determines, this ambiguity can be clarified by the reader's method of critical interpretation, an interpretation whose "understanding" is compatible with the fictions in Crane's entire war canon, then a new critical methodology is called for. *Red Badge* is in need of a theoretical framework, one which views this novel as a part of the continuum of Crane's war fiction canon, as a novel whose motifs are developed and interwoven throughout Crane's canon of war fiction, as a novel whose thematic intention is part and parcel of Crane's comprehensive purpose for his entire war fiction canon. I wish to offer satire as a practical and necessary critical tool to study Fleming's apparent development as a hero. Hence, I propose that Henry Fleming's heroics, dramatizations of contemporary romanticized notions of heroism, are actually satirical ploys orchestrated by Crane to allow the reader to appreciate the absurdity of traditional notions of heroism.

The critics' failure to use Crane's entire canon of war fictions to explicate *The Red Badge of Courage* has resulted, as Holton indicates, in contradictions between "seemingly sound assertions" about individual stories. Yet in Crane's war fiction canon, we can identify patterns of actions and belief that are consistently affirmed or negated: Crane's authentic position serves as a static buttress for his war fiction, and Crane's attack dynamically develops from a light-hearted Horatian satire on romanticized notions of traditional heroism to a biting and bitter Juvenalian satire directed toward the absurdity of romanticized notions of heroism. In fact the earlier and later war fictions are uniquely reciprocal in confirming the main object of Crane's satire, to criticize in order to correct. As the earlier fictions, whose attack is implicit, inculcate Crane's moral norms, so the later war fictions, which furnish a direct and incisive attack, depend upon the earlier fiction to delineate Crane's authentic position. However, since much of the gentle and humorous satire is implied in such earlier fictions as *Red Badge*, viewing this novel, a part of a continuum of twenty-four war fictions, from the hindsight of later war stories whose attack is more direct and severe, more explicitly reveals Crane's thematic purpose: to attack notions of romanticized heroism and affirm Crane's personal concept of heroism. Later works which reveal Crane's disdain for romanticized conventional notions of heroism, for example, graphically dramatize the stark realization of glorified heroism by the image of the "plop"[9] as the dirt is thrown on the "chalk-blue" corpse in "The Upturned Face" and by the shout of the solders in "The Kicking Twelfth," who cry out after their initial "victorious" battle, "My God, we're all cut to pieces" (6:295).

In its purest form Crane's concept of heroism embraces kindness or compassion which Crane identifies in a letter to Nellie Crouse as "the final wall in the wise man's thoughts."[10] This "Human Kindness," the dominant element of Crane's moral commitment, embodies the basis of Crane's authentic position, the primary standard on which *Red Badge* rests. Such a position tacitly affirms that Crane is sympathetic and not indifferent toward his subject.[11] Buttressed by Crane's convictions, Crane's personal concept of heroism undergirds and governs *Red Badge*. Aspects of this personal concept of heroism are dramatized throughout Crane's war fiction as ethical applications of Crane's moral commitment. Also, although *Red Badge* uses various characters to portray different aspects of Crane's personal heroism, characters in the shorter war fiction singly dramatize a phase of Crane's concept of heroism. In this manner, Crane's shorter war fiction presents characters who become heroes by exercising their personal responsibility, if only momentarily, as Little Nell, whose heroism is dramatized in "small things—of no consequence and yet warming" (6:147) in "God Rest Ye Merry Gentlemen"; and Lige Wigram, who in "Virtue in War" compassionately and self-sacrificially aids Gates, who has previously repelled Lige's friendly advances.

I will offer Edward Rosenheim's theoretical model as a pragmatic critical methodology for identifying the parameters of satire: "satire consists of an attack by means of a manifest fiction upon discernible historic particulars."[12] This attack directs the narrative, whose primary purpose is not to narrate but rather explicitly to criticize a "particular" that has an historical referent and implicitly to teach a lesson."[13] Thus satire interplays a direct critical attack with an indirect affirmation. This affirmation or norm, which identifies the writer's authentic position "in terms of [his] authentic feelings and attitudes" and beliefs, "disclose[s] the precise nature of the fictional posture, the degree to which it departs from the satirist's authentic position, [and] the nature of the authentic position itself."[14] While the norm provides the criteria for judging satire and determining the connotative meaning of the narrative, the satiric techniques which produce distortion and incongruency to reinforce the attack suggest that the denotative meaning in the story should be identified as "manifest fiction," a "fictional posture" which departs from "literal truth" and replaces it with "satiric fiction."[15] Moreover, the satirist intends for the reader to recognize the fiction for what it is because, according to Rosenheim, "Fiction serves a satiric purpose only when we are aware of the manner and extent of its departure" from the satirist's authentic position.[16] Finally, the satirist must appear to be detached from the subject he seeks to criticize and change; else he may be accused of sanctimoniousness or bitterness, either of which could cause the reader to sympathize with the satiric victim.

Hence, to identify *Red Badge* as satire, the reader should first be vigilant of the satiric techniques, specifically irony, which reveals the "manifest fiction" and as such alerts the reader to the possibility of satire. Coupled with his recognition of this narrative's "manifest fiction," the reader should also acknowledge Crane's authentic position which implicitly undergirds this narrative and provides the criteria for judging *Red Budge*. The reader should recognize the incongruency between Crane's authentic position, manifested in dramatizations of aspects of Crane's personal concept of heroism in this novel and throughout Crane's war fiction, and Crane's dramatizations of the traditional romantizied concept of heroism, implicitly dramatized in *Red Badge* and explicitly undercut in later war fictions. The ironical juxtaposition of these disparate conceptions of heroism suggests that Crane's denotative depiction of the traditional notion of heroism, actually the referent for the contemporary social milieu and attitudes, is being attacked and must therefore be recognized as "manifest fiction."

The sources of Crane's "historical particulars," referents for contemporary romanticized notions of heroism, emanate from the 1890s, a period of "war consciousness and war preparation"[17] that "echoed with the cry of Manifest Destiny."[18] This predominant war sentiment, the "distinguishing trait of the American character," was expressed by John Hay in a letter written on July 27, 1898 during the Spanish American War: "It has been a splendid little war, begun with the highest motives, carried on with magnificent intelligence and spirit, favored by that Fortune which loves the brave."[19] This imperialistic attitude of "splendid little war[s]" which swept the nation into the Spanish American War, according to Edwin Cady,[20] is confirmed by Richard Harding Davis, a Spanish-American war correspondent, who wrote that "war as it is conducted at this end of the century is civilized."[21] Perhaps the chief proponent of this imperialistic attitude which glorified war was Theodore Roosevelt, who, according to Pizer, viewed America's "expansionist activities as a duty-bound extension of our heritage of freedom."[22]

According to Thomas Gullason, "No American writer was a more ardent anti-imperialist, a more serious defiant, sincere humanitarian than Stephen Crane."[23] Crane's disdain for imperialistic attitudes which idealize war, heroism, and journalistic duplicity may be generally attributed to his experiences as a war correspondent in 1897 and 1898 during the Greco-Turkish and Spanish-American Wars. These experiences allowed him personally to view the actual war and thus to see behind the romantic, imperialistic facade. As a result of these experiences, Crane was torn between depicting his personal observation of the hell of war and acquiescing to the demands of the newspaper editor who paid him to present "hair-raising dispatches, bombastic scoops on heroism"[24] in a steady flow of news dispatches, which Crane refers to in a poem as a "collection of half injustices."[25] Crane's contempt for this type of journalistic duplicity is evident in "Roosevelt's Rough Riders' Loss Due to a Gallant Blunder." Throughout this war dispatch, in a mock-heroic manner Crane depicts the incompetence of the actions of these Rough Riders; the oxymoron "Gallant Blunder" in the title indicates the absurdity of inflated news reporting. Moreover, in his newspaper article "The Blue Badge of Cowardice," Crane implies his disdain for the imperialistic attitude by his sympathy for the physical suffering caused by the war: "Their plight makes a man hate himself for being well fed and having some place to go . . . I wish I knew what is to become of these poor people."[26]

A close scrutiny of *Red Badge* reveals that irony is the primary technique which alerts the reader to the fictive nature of this narrative's denotative meaning. The main textual clues which allow the reader to recognize this irony are clashes between idealized and realistic notions of heroism. The socially-sanctioned notion of heroism portrayed in this novel views war as a series of "pictures of glory," "Greek-like struggles," and "mighty deeds of arms," which greedily anticipate "great things" (pp. 66, 8, 8, 19). In fact, one unidentified character in this novel celebrates war as "Everybody fightin'. Blood and destruction . . . Whoop-a-dadee" (p. 92). However, in *Red Badge* and later war fictions, Crane uses the motley assortment of incongruous and grotesque details of the reality of war to express moral outrage against the unbearable discordance of the traditional war code. In *Red Badge* the horrors, madness, and "chaos" (p. 32) of the war are initially depicted when a soldier falls down; as he reaches for his rifle, a "comrade, unseeing, trod upon his hand" (p. 16) and crunches his fingers. Throughout this novel appear descriptions of "torn bodies which expressed the awful machinery in which the men had been entangled" (p. 52). A soldier sings as he marches: "Sing a song 'a vic'try / A pocketful 'a bullets / Five an' twenty dead men / Baked in a—pie" (p. 51). War is referred to as "the red animal," which the "blood-swollen god, would have bloated fill" (p. 69), and the regiment, which "left a coherent trail of bodies" (p. 105), is derogatorily likened to "one of those moving monsters wending with many feet." A similar depiction of the battalion as a "loom, clinking clanking, plinking, to weave . . . the cloth of death" (6:109) is presented in "The Price of the Harness." Such later war fictions as "The Clan

of No-Name," "The Upturned Face," "And If He Wills, We Must Die," and
"An Episode of War," also detail graphic details of the senseless horrors of
war. Such horrors undercut idealized notions of heroism, which should be
viewed as "manifest fiction." However, Crane is not indifferent as he objec-
tively relates these senseless horrors of war, but rather deeply concerned and
morally outraged, for the chaos and horror of war do not accord with Crane's
personal standards.

Crane's norms are explicitly and implicitly dramatized in *The Red Badge
of Courage*. Ethical applications of aspects of Crane's heroic ideal are explicitly
verbalized by the narrator and Henry Fleming's mother, who looks

> with some contempt upon the quality of his [Henry's] war-ardor
> and patriotism. She could . . . give him many hundreds of reasons
> why he was of vastly more importance on the farm than on the
> field of battle . . . [H]er statements on the subject came from a deep
> conviction. (pp. 5–6)

Similar to Crane's intense disdain for "war-ardor," Fleming's mother's
ethical convictions reveal a contempt for the romanticized social notions
of heroism. Crane's norms are also explicitly verbalized by the narrator.
In his brief commentary regarding Fleming's regiment in one of its final
battles, the narrator's bifocal, value-laden comment ironically juxtaposes the
importance of reputation with actual survival and in this manner affirms
the insignificance of the former: "It is difficult to think of reputation when
others were thinking of skins" (p. 112). Kindness and compassion, elements
of Crane's personal concept of heroism, are implicitly dramatized in *Red
Badge* by the tattered man, the man with the cheery voice, Wilson, and the
sarcastic man. The tattered man, who is reminiscent of the later incarnation
of Henry Fleming in "The Veteran," is more concerned for the mortally
wounded Jim Conklin and the uninjured Fleming than for his own health.
Even as the tattered man is forced to admit, "I don't believe I kin walk much
furder," in his ensuing sentence he observes, "Yeh [Fleming] looks pretty
peek-ed yerself, . . . I bet yeh've gota worser one [injury] than yeh think. Yed
better take keer of yer hurt" (pp. 60–61). However, because the tattered man
innocently inquires the location of Fleming's wound, questions which "had
been knife-thrusts" to Fleming's egotism, Fleming, unlike Lige Wigram in
"Virtue in War," deserts the tattered man, who then wanders "about helplessly in the fields" (p. 62). Like the tattered man, the man with the cheery
voice, who befriends Fleming and guides him back to camp, seeks no recognition for his kindness: "[I]t suddenly occurred to the youth that he had
not once seen his face" (p. 74). Wilson's actions also embody kindness and

selflessness. When Fleming returns to the camp, Wilson cares for him as would an "amateur nurse." Wilson gives his only blanket to Fleming, makes "his patient [Henry] drink largely from the canteen that contains the coffee" (p. 78), and bandages Fleming's wound (p. 77). Likewise the sarcastic man, who chides Fleming for his vanity and desire for public acclaim, affirms Crane's personal concept of heroism because the sarcastic man recognizes that kindness can only be realized when its viewpoint is eccentric: After a defeat in one of Fleming's final skirmishes, Fleming "grandly and decisively" rails out against his superiors (p. 91). But the "sarcastic man who was tramping at the youth's side" observes: "Mebbe yeh think yeh fit th' hull battle yestirday, Flemin" (p. 91). The sarcastic man's observation seems to echo Fleming's mother's reminder, "Don't go a-thinkin' yeh kin lick th' hull rebel army at the start, because yeh can't. Yer jest one little feller 'mongst a hull lot'a others" (p. 7).

The romanticized conventional notion of heroism is primarily dramatized from the viewpoint of Henry Fleming, the chief satiric victim, who considers himself to possess attributes which he actually lacks. Fleming epitomizes the imperialistic posture which applauds the notion that has "glorious triumphs" and embraces the social recognition of greatness as an end in itself. The extent to which Fleming's beliefs and actions deviate from Crane's norms as Fleming strives for some degree of manhood or "heroism" may be identified throughout the novel. At the outset Fleming's beliefs do not accord with his desires; however, as the novel develops, Fleming's desires and beliefs finally reflect only the traditional idealized concept of heroism. It is from this final stance that Fleming can declare that he is a man, a hero. However, when Fleming conceives of himself as a traditional hero, he has become the chief victim of Crane's satire and Crane's primary means of revealing the sham, ludicrousness, and inhumanity of the traditional concept of heroism.

In juxtaposed paragraphs in the opening pages of this novel, Fleming unknowingly discredits himself by unintentionally revealing the incongruity between his desires and beliefs. In the first of these paragraphs, Fleming acknowledges that the traditional concept of heroism with its depictions of thrilling "bloody conflicts" (p. 5) is no longer viable, and great battles are now relegated to the past since "Men were better, or, more timid" (p. 5). However, in the subsequent paragraph Fleming appears to embrace this traditional notion, as he burns to enlist in order to experience firsthand these great battles with "breathless deeds" (p. 5). In fact, shortly afterwards, Fleming admits as he leaves his mother that he felt "suddenly ashamed of his purposes" (p. 8), which are manifested in his desire to follow the traditional code of heroism.

As the story develops, Fleming vacillates between an acceptance and rejection of the traditional notion of heroism. Initially he primarily continues to question the speciousness of the traditional concept of heroism: Fleming observes the forward-moving brigade which "was hurrying briskly to be gulped into the infernal mouth of the war-god"; he wonders if they are "some wondrous breed" or "fools" (p. 43). However, in Chapter Eleven, Fleming's beliefs and desires begin to embrace chiefly the traditional concept of heroism: Fleming felt he "was convicted by himself of many shameful crimes against the gods of tradition" (p. 14); and shortly afterward Henry so fully embraces the traditional notion of heroism that he "thought that he wished he was dead. He believed that he envied a corpse," who could "receive laurels from tradition" before they, unlike he, "had had opportunities to flee" (p. 67). Yet immediately Fleming incongruously accepts and rejects at once the traditional notion of heroism: "He cried out bitterly that their crowns were stolen and their robes of glorious memories were shams. However, he still said that it was a great pity he was not as they" (p. 67).

As Fleming's beliefs increasingly focus on the traditional concept of heroism, Fleming's recovered "pride" (pp. 9, 115, 117, 122, 129), "self-satisfaction," conception of himself as a "fine fellow" (p. 39), and public acclaim—all seemingly necessary attributes of Fleming's concept of manhood—become increasingly dominant. For example, Fleming's chief concern after he runs is his public image. On several occasions Fleming seems to view "self-pride" and "public recognition" as prerequisites for "manfulness": "His self-pride was now entirely restored ... and allowed no thoughts of his own to keep him from an attitude of manfulness. He had performed his mistakes in the dark, so he was still a man" (p. 86). Moreover, vanity is useful to Fleming as a means of establishing his public image: "if he himself could believe in his virtuous perfection, he conceived that there would be small trouble in convincing all others" (p. 66). The symbiotic relationship between vanity and manhood is suggested in the following statement: "They gazed about them with looks of uplifted pride, feeling new trust in the grim, always confident weapons in their hands. And they were men" (p. 115). However, pride and desire for public acclaim are constituents of the traditional concept of heroism, not Crane's personal concept of heroism.

The meaninglessness of the self-centered notion of heroism which is determined by public acclaim is depicted in such war stories as "God Rest Ye, Merry Gentlemen" by the newspaper's sensational news, "The Revenge of the *Adolphus*" by the erroneous news report, and "The Clan of No-Name" by the Spanish Colonel's office report. Reputation is also a primary concern of various characters in Crane's war fiction. For example, Caspar Cadogan, the epitome of the traditional notion of heroism, is finally undercut in "The Second Generation." On the other hand, humility, an eccentric quality in keeping with Crane's norms, is dramatized in such war fictions as "War Memories" by the Regulars, the unsung heroes who charge up San Juan Hill, and by Admiral Simpson, a "great man" whose actions tacitly affirm "plain, pure, unsauced accomplishment" (6:240).

Increasingly self-centered, Fleming finally embraces only the traditional notions of heroism: "It was revealed to him that he had been a barbarian, a beast. He had fought like a pagan ... and he was now what he called a hero ... He had slept and, awakening, found himself a knight" (p. 97). By Fleming's skewed equation of fighting like a "barbarian, a beast" with being a "hero," a "knight," Fleming reveals the single focus of his actions and beliefs. Unlike the opening paragraphs in which he embraced the traditional notion only in his dreams, "But awake he regarded battles as crimson blotches on the pages of the past" (p. 5), in this passage Fleming "awakening" now adopts completely the romanticized notion of heroism. Similarly, in "Three Miraculous Soldiers" Mary initially equates her romantic notions of heroism with "dreaming" (6:33).

In the closing scene Crane immediately forces the self-satisfied and self-centered Henry Fleming to confront the dramatization of Crane's personal concept of heroism, personified by the selfless concern and kindness of the tattered man. This confrontation implicitly suggests the hypocrisy and superficiality of the traditional concept of heroism: Recalling his desertion of the tattered man, a "vision of cruelty brooded over" Fleming and "darkened his view of the deeds in purple and gold" (p. 134). In fact, "For a time, this pursuing recollection of the tattered man took all elation from the youth's veins. Yet gradually he mustered force to put the sin at a distance" (p. 135).

In his final satirical deduction, Fleming erroneously pronounces that "He was a man" (p. 135) because he has survived the heat of two skirmishes on his second and final day of actual fighting. Hence, he will never again "quail before his guides wherever they should point" (p. 5). This deduction, which employs exaggeration and superlatives falsely to assume that Fleming may predetermine his actions for all time because of a brief, successful encounter with heavy enemy fire, conflicts with the outcome of other war fictions. In fact, as other war fictions indicate, the same character may display bravery on one occasion but subsequently lapse into cowardice or vanity, such as in "The Grey Sleeve," in which the brave and heretofore respected Union captain later discredits himself in the eyes of his men by his actions toward the girl.

The closing lines of the story implicitly suggest the meaninglessness of the traditional concept of heroism by ironically juxtaposing the point of view of the romanticized concept of war, adopted by the safe and self-satisfied Fleming, who "saw that the world was a world for him," with the actual result of battle, portrayed by the "despondent," wounded, "weary," and those who would never return (p. 135). When Crane was an international celebrity and in a position, like Fleming, to assume that "the world was a world for him," Crane chose instead to "remain true" to his standards and compassionately empathize with the "labor and sorrow" of life,"[27] the "bedraggled train" of "weary" and "despondent" soldiers (p. 135), for Crane acknowledged that "There is more of this sort of thing [human agony] in war than glory . . . flags, banners, shouting, and victory" (9:56). A letter Crane wrote to Nellie Crouse seems to confirm Crane's belief that "life" consists largely of "labor and sorrow" rather than "tranquil skies, fresh meadows, cool breezes . . . and eternal peace" (p. 135).

A consideration of *The Red Badge of Courage* as a satiric novel resolves the ambiguity acknowledged in much of the previous criticism. This novel, which attacks the romanticized notion of heroism and commends the qualities manifested in Crane's personal concept of heroism, allows the reader to identify Henry Fleming as an unreliable character who is finally a pawn and exemplar of the traditional notion of heroism. Such a reading suggests that Crane breaks with the traditional conventions of the nineteenth-century realistic war novel whose critics view Henry as assuming finally "a store of inner strength and conviction," a characteristic of the developmental novel.[28] Since Crane employs Horatian satire in *Red Badge*, the attack is indirect and comparatively light-hearted; however, the primary satiric target of this novel, the romanticized notion of heroism, is explicitly and bitterly attacked as a meaningless and absurd attitude which creates the confusion of war in Crane's later fictions.

I have employed Rosenheim's model as a useful theoretical paradigm. However, regardless of the model used, the essential elements of satire are inherent in Crane's war fiction: a satiric attack or criticism which implies a satiric victim, a satiric fiction which suggests historical particulars in disguise; norms or standards which imply a social milieu; and rhetorical techniques which may identify and reinforce the attack. Employing satire as a theoretical base allows for an appreciation of the development of identifiable patterns of thoughts and actions which are consistently affirmed or negated throughout Crane's war fiction. Such patterns or motifs suggest the thematic intention or "center" of Crane's war fiction, to encourage the reader to appreciate the inhumanity of romanticized notions of war and to affirm a "kinder, gentler" heroism. Moreover, I believe Crane's war fictions are mutually informative: together they provide clear manifestations of historical referents, Crane's personal concept of heroism, and distorted aspects of romanticized traditional heroism—the crucial tools of satire.[29] By informing individual war fictions, as *Red Badge*, and at the same time allowing a coherent and comprehensive thematic understanding that accords with Crane's entire war canon, satire serves as a necessary critical methodology that addresses the concerns of Edwin Cady and other influential critics of Stephen Crane's works.

Notes

1. Edwin W. Cady, *Stephen Crane*, rev. ed., Twayne's United States Authors Series 23 (Boston: Twayne, 1980), p. 17.

2. Milne Holton, *Cylinder of Vision: The Fiction and Journalistic Writings of Stephen Crane* (Baton Rouge: Louisiana State Univ. Press, 1972), p. 5.

3. Stephen Crane, *The Red Badge of Courage*. Vol. 2 of *The Works of Stephen Crane* (Charlottesville: Univ. Press of Virginia, 1969–73), p. 97. Subsequent references to this text will be cited parenthetically by page number.

4. Joseph X. Brennan, "Stephen Crane and the Limits of Irony," *Criticism* 11 (1969): 184.

5. Donald Pizer, "A Primer of Fictional Aesthetics," *College English* 30 (1969): 576.

6. Steven Mailloux, *Interpretive Conventions: The Reader in the Study of American Fiction* (Ithaca, NY: Cornell Univ. Press, 1982), pp. 195–96.

7. Donald Pizer, "*The Red Badge of Courage*: Text, Theme, and Form," *South Atlantic Quarterly* 84 (1985): 302–13.

8. Stephen Crane, *The Correspondence of Stephen Crane*, eds. Stanley Wertheim and Paul Sorrentino (New York: Columbia Univ. Press, 1988), p. 323.

9. Stephen Crane, *Tales of War*, Vol. 6 of *The Works of Stephen Crane* (Charlottesville: Univ. Press of Virginia, 1969–75), p. 300, hereafter cited parenthetically in the text by volume and page.

10. *The Correspondence of Stephen Crane*, p. 180.

11. Crane's concept of heroism appears to extend beyond the superficial traditional concept, as demonstrated in the following poem:

("Tell brave deeds of war."
Then they recounted tales,
"There were stern stands
And bitter runs for glory."
Ah, I think there were braver deeds

(Stephen Crane, *Poems and Literary Remains*, Vol. 10 of *The Works of Stephen Crane*, ed. Fredson Bowers, 10 vols. [Charlottesville: The Univ. Press of Virginia, 1969–75], p. 10). Subsequent documentation will be given within the text by volume and page.

12. Edward W. Rosenheim, Jr., *Swift and the Satirist's Art* (Chicago: Univ. of Chicago Press, 1963), p. 31.

13. Rosenheim, pp. 179–80, 6, 18.

14. Rosenheim, pp. 179–80, 21.

15. Rosenheim, p. 17.

16. Rosenheim, p. 179.

17. Alfred Kazin, *An American Procession* (New York: Knopf, 1984), p. 265.

18. Thomas A. Gullason, "Stephen Crane: Anti-Imperialist," *American Literature* 30 (1958): 237.

19. Quoted by Kazin, p. 266.

20. Cady, p. 89.

21. Quoted by R. W. Stallman, *Stephen Crane* (New York: Braziller, 1968), p. 352.

22. Donald Pizer, "The War as Catalyst," *American Thought and Writing: The 1890's*, ed. Donald Pizer (Boston: Houghton, 1972), p. 447.

23. Gullason, p. 237.

24. Stallman, p. 359.

25. Stephen Crane, "a newspaper is a collection of half-injustices," *Poems and Literary Remains*, Vol. 10 of *The Works of Stephen Crane*, ed. Fredson Bowers, 10 vols. (Charlottesville: The Univ. Press of Virginia, 1969–75), p. 52. Subsequent documentation will be given within the text as volume and page.

26. Stephen Crane, "The Blue Badge of Cowardice," *Reports of War*, Vol. 9 of *The Works of Stephen Crane* (Charlottesville: Univ. Press of Virginia, 1969–75). p.41, hereafter cited parenthetically by volume and page.

27. *The Correspondence of Stephen Crane*, p. 187.

28. Pizer, "*The Red Badge of Courage*: Text, Theme, and Form," p. 307.

29. These ideas are developed more fully in Mary Ann Shaw, "Stephen Crane's Concept of Heroism: Satire in the War Stories of Stephen Crane," Diss. Texas A & M Univ., 1985.

PHILIP D. BEIDLER

Stephen Crane's The Red Badge of Courage: Henry Fleming's Courage in Its Contexts

After nearly a century of interpretive debate, criticism of *The Red Badge of Courage* has not yet talked about the courage of Henry Fleming in its particular historical contexts.[1] By the latter phrase, I mean specifically the contexts of cultural assumption and value that may be said to have defined courage for the common soldier of the American Civil War and also, in large part, through the complex dynamics of cultural memory, for the young Stephen Crane who decided to write a novel about it a generation later. To put the matter more simply, much of the ongoing debate over "answers" to the central problem posed in *The Red Badge of Courage* remains due in large measure, I believe, to our inability, from our own perspectives of culture, literary *and* historical, to remember how to ask what would have seemed at the time a number of pertinent and even obvious questions. What, for instance, might "courage" have generally meant to an average young Civil War volunteer of humble, upright origins? Of more particular importance, how did such "courage" come to be represented in the anecdotal reminiscences of veterans and in popular postwar texts such as *Battles and Leaders of the Civil War* which we know to have served for Crane as primary sources?[2] To what degree, for instance, did an idea of "courage," based on a complex legacy of pre-war values, not only seem to have survived the shock of battle but now also to have become re-enshrined in cultural memory, both North

From *CLIO* 20, no. 3 (Spring 1991): 235–51. Copyright © 1991 by Henry Kozicki.

and South, as a form of collective heroic nostalgia; and to what extent and in what cultural forms had such an idea now transmitted itself into the thoughts and values of the work's contemporary readers? To read *The Red Badge of Courage* in light of such questions as these, I would propose, is to know most fully the work that Stephen Crane wrote and that his audience read; and it is also to contextualize the long interpretive tradition arising out of that work on the necessary ground of its own complex historicity as well.

The primary impetus for this essay lies not in literary studies but in recent developments in military history and historiography attempting to re-envision what John Keegan has called the face of battle within the combatants' likely assumptions of cultural meaning and value. Specifically, I am indebted to two American texts in this vein, Gerald F. Lindermann's *Embattled Courage* and Reid Mitchell's *Civil War Soldiers*,[3] both unprecedented in their penetration into the consciousness of the actual Civil War combatant—what Mitchell calls "the psychology of service"—in all dimensions of the experience: the values and concepts of manly action carried into the war by individual soldiers; the gradual unraveling of convictions in the face of fear, privation, injury, illness, death; the eventual displacement in memory (as treated in particular detail by Lindermann) of the grim vision of the battlefield by nostalgic images of long-ago excitement and heroics. Accordingly, as studies of personal *and* cultural transformation in Civil War combatants, both provide illuminating insights into the national consciousness ranging far beyond the war itself into the mythic fibre of late nineteenth-century American life at large. And not the least of these forms of illumination, I would propose, is the important new light in which they allow us to read that late nineteenth-century literary masterpiece of war and personal and cultural transformation, *The Red Badge of Courage*.

* * *

"He was a man."[4] Occurring on the last page of *The Red Badge of Courage*, this simple sentence has remained for nearly a century the focus of debate over the ultimate meaning of Henry Fleming's "courage." And justly so. For even to the most credulous reader, given the evolution of consciousness depicted in the work—replete with its false starts, misguided rationalizations, petty deceits, and makeshift complacencies—such a concluding remark could not have been attended to without some deep sense of ironist accommodation. That reader would have already noted, for instance, a similar usage to describe the quite momentary elation of soldiers in the midst of a hopelessly confused action of charge, repulse, and counter-charge. "The impetus of enthusiasm was theirs again," the narrator has told us breathlessly. "They gazed about them with looks of uplifted pride, feeling new trust in the grim, always confident weapons in their hands. And they were men" (94). And as to Henry himself, after he has returned to his unit with his secret of cowardice masked by the badge of his wounding, the exact phrasing has marked the status of his moral manhood at nothing less than its exact moral nadir. "He had performed his mistakes in the dark," the narrator puts it succinctly, "so he was still a man" (72).

Yet as Mitchell's and Lindermann's studies make clear, in the matter of commonplace moral terminology, that reader would have at least been able to "stabilize" the irony within a relatively familiar context of cultural interpretation. Most importantly, this would certainly have been the case as to the pivotal inscription of the word "man" into the larger cultural discourse of "courage." For in a vast number of cases, as to both ethics and semantics, "men may very well have fought during the Civil War," writes Mitchell, "for reasons having less to do with ideology" in any particular sense "than with masculine identity." He cites an Illinois soldier's assertion to his mother that "coming into this war has made a man of your son." And from a Confederate, he correspondingly quotes the belief, recently born of battle "that he is a Man and is in a Man's place" (18). Indeed, on both sides, "manliness," if not exactly equated with courage, was terminologically one of the chief stars in the constellation of values of which, for the Civil War soldier, the latter concept may be said to have consisted. It was not at all unusual, Lindermann points out, for soldiers to use "'courage' and 'manhood' interchangeably" (8).

So for that matter, Lindermann goes on, might they have also associated both of these terms with another, "godliness," as well. In fact, precisely "as courage and godliness were linked, so were cowardice and disbelief" (10). According to Lindermann, at the highest levels of association, "godliness" could on the battlefield truly induce a sense of Divine protection utterly displacing any feeling of "fear for one's safety" (9). In Mitchell's version, "American Christians were particularly prone to attribute escape from death in battle to providential intervention, the result of prayer and devotion" (78). At the level of common morality, "godliness" operated in a widespread conviction that a virtuous army would naturally be a victorious army. Again, as Mitchell notes, and in terms echoed within the novel by Henry's own mother, a chief "contradiction experienced by the soldier was that between his image of the volunteer as the preeminently virtuous patriot and the reality of the men with whom he shared army life. Where he had expected to find paragons, he found mortal men. Both the Union and Confederate armies had their share of petty thieves, drunkards, slackers, and other lowlife" (73). Or, as one particularly demoralized Confederate moralist put it in a letter from camp, "I haven't heard a sermon in I can't tell when. You hear no more talk about religion here than if there was no such thing. The army is more demoralizing than I ever dreamed of. Three-fourths I recon, of the officers and men in this Regiment are profane swearers and card players" (74).

A third, if somewhat more amorphous adjunct to "manliness" and "god-liness" in the crown of "courage" would have been "Duty," defined perhaps most generally as manly perseverance. And a fourth, and final one, at least for the common soldier ("Knightliness" appears to have been reserved mainly for officers),[5] would have been "Honor," a term perhaps more quaint and obscure than any other to the twentieth-century mind, yet to a nineteenth-century predecessor still in many ways—particularly in terms of the haze of romantic retrospection with which the war eventually came to be invested—as clear, according to Lindermann, as its definition in the dictionary: "True noble-ness of mind; magnanimity; dignified respect for a character, springing from probity, principle, or moral rectitude; a distinguishing trait in the character of *good men*" (11). And nowhere, moreover, did this particular "linkage between honor and courage" reveal itself more regularly and pervasively, he goes on, than in "Civil War soldiers' frequent references to the 'honorable death'—inevitably the courageous death—and the 'honorable wound'—inevitably suffered in the course of courageous action" (12).

These assumptions of value and belief, Mitchell and Lindermann go on to demonstrate, would eventually find challenge and negation on a scale commensurate to the slaughter of the young men who carried them into Civil War combat. The conflict quickly became a modern war of massed technology and wholesale terror and destruction. Apace, soldiers often unlearned earlier, inherited values and beliefs and bent their wits mainly on survival. Yet once home at the war's end, as Lindermann particularly points out, they quickly seem to have become "subject to an acceleration of selective memory, that strong psychological propensity to suppress the painful" (267). This tendency in turn was augmented by a revival of martial pride in the 1880s and 1890s attributable to a new, expansive spirit of nationalism and geopolitical mission. By 1898, Lindermann concludes, "the values young men carried to war . . . were again those of 1861" (297). At the dawning of a new century, "Civil War veterans had become symbols of changelessness—but only by obliterating or amending an experience of combat so convulsive that it had for a time cut the cord of experience" (297).

* * *

As I hope this summary has shown, these texts present the student of *The Red Badge of Courage* with an unprecedented interpretive opportunity, for

they now open up the possibility of discussing the courage of Henry Fleming in its nineteenth-century American contexts within a historiographic
matrix of almost mathematical exactitude. Although Crane was writing
the novel thirty years after the fact, there can be no doubt that one of his
primary intentions was to recreate, literarily, the actual values, expectations,
and experiences of a typical common soldier confronted with the actualities
of Civil War combat. As noted earlier, he avidly consulted the reminiscences
of veterans, and his main "objective" source was indisputably the *Battles and
Leaders* series published in *Century*, by general consent the primary popular
organ of a nascent military revivalism. By 1895, even as the young nostal-
gist-naturalist sought faithfully to reproduce for his readers the values of the
Civil War soldier against the backdrop of new, subversive literary-cultural
ideologies, he also remained part of his own culture, one that in fact had
re-established those older values and beliefs upon the altar of popular faith.

* * *

To turn to the text proper of *The Red Badge of Courage* in the relatively new
context of social history opened up by works such as Mitchell and Lindermann's is to see an old work with an eerie sense of new encounter. It is as
if one has been supplied with certain answers to a whole set of interpretive
questions that strangely had not occurred; yet now they seem the main ones
immediately worth asking.

The title alone, for instance, read in its social-historical contexts, becomes
a central case in point. Most twentieth-century readers, one suddenly sees,
have received it—and in the process have established their context for reading the work it announces—as something that cannot be read *in and of itself*
as anything other than ironic. The quaint figure of a "red badge," we think,
combining with what seems the idea of "courage" as an equally quaint and
idealized moral abstraction, must surely be announcing a familiar self-inter-
rogation. In contrast, such might not have been the automatic expectation
for a reader steeped in nineteenth-century conventions of courage and in its
particular association with the idea of the noble wound, not to mention one
who, in a relatively short retrospect as wars go, had also just taken in a subtitle
that read "An Episode of the American Civil War." Rather, the title might
then have acquired its most profound ironic suggestions as the text develops *precisely* in the fact that it could have been read initially, one might dare
to speculate, as quite plausibly unironic, a title that seems to mean mainly
what it says.[6] Indeed, the logic of such literalism *is* the dramatic logic of the
text: of the dishonorable circumstances in which this particular red badge of
courage is earned—by a confused coward in drifting flight struck down by

a coward in full flight acting in full frenzy of his cowardice; and of the correspondingly dishonest uses to which it is afterward put by the soldier who has received it as contrasted with the noble construction put upon it by his fellows. And Henry, for his subsequent deviousness and even cynicism, is in this respect the truest believer. He desperately wants, and believes things will all come right because of, "a red badge of courage" (46). Or, failing that, in his moment of darkest despair, he sees himself killed upon the battlefield and, Tom Sawyer-like, imagines "the magnificent pathos of his dead body" (55).[7] What is crucial, then, to our reading of this irony—and of Henry's capacity for private dishonesty and public deceit as a consequence of his cowardice—is our realization that he knows none of his fellows is likely to associate a visible wound with anything other than courage. The question, we see, would simply not have occurred to them. And it is *this cultural fact*—this fact of cultural assumption, the fact of the wound itself as titular and dramatic signifier, as we see, that will dictate the logic, once Henry has committed his initial act of cowardice, of the whole train of encounter eventuating in his return to his unit and his achieving of a kind of final heroism.

Yet other, preparatory "contextualizations" of such a particular idea of "courage" announce themselves in the text from the first pages onward. A simple, albeit crucial early example, for instance, is the relentless identification of a single quite specific source for Henry Fleming's deep psychological discomfiture on the eve of battle. His particular question, the "more serious problem" that has made him retire in solitude from his comrades' collective agitation, we suddenly see, is only one of many that might have occurred to another soldier in another war at another time. "He tried to mathematically prove to himself" the narrator tells us succinctly, "that he would not run from a battle" (11). Indeed, such a "problem" seems rather less likely than some others that might seem more obvious. He does not ask whether he will be killed. He does not ask whether he will suffer a painful wound and be maimed or crippled. He does not even ask exactly—in a work by a man who, as we know, was himself obsessed by the question of physical courage—if he will be brave. What he specifically asks, rather, is whether he will prove visibly incapable of *doing his duty*. For, as Mitchell again reminds us, it was a particular signature of this war that "many soldiers awaited their first battle impatiently; they felt eager to prove their courage and defeat the enemy" (75). And exactly this, during the whole five chapters of preparation that follow, remains the thing endlessly reiterated as the source of Henry's "problem" (11, 19, 25), his "debate" (16), his "troubles" (25). It is really, we see, even in the first of the work's great metaphysically portentous scenes, involving Henry's first glimpse of a dead enemy soldier lying on the path of march, the proximate cause of all the larger mystery, the question, so to speak, behind the Question:

> The youth looked keenly at the ashen face. The wind raised the
> tawny beard. It moved as if a hand were stroking it. He vaguely
> desired to walk around and around the body and stare; the impulse
> of the living to try and read in dead eyes the answer to the
> Question. (22)

What had it been like, he seems to ask the corpse? Had he, in the hour of
his dying, acquitted himself as a man?[8]

Thus, repeatedly, Henry asks in one way or another not whether he will
die, whether he will suffer painful wounds, whether he will be brave or scared,
but whether he will run. What I want to emphasize is that this is hardly an
obvious question for us; but for Henry, given the contexts of his culture, it is
not only the obvious one but the only one that matters. Moreover, what small
comfort he receives in his early anxieties, predictably from the "good" and
"manly" Jim Conklin, and also surprisingly, a short while afterward, from the
vain and childish Wilson, is posed repeatedly in these quite specific terms of
cultural group ethos. "How do you think the reg'ment 'll do?" Henry asks Jim.
"Think any of the boys 'll run?" (12). "I think they'll fight better than some, if
worse than others. That's what I figger," Jim replies. "They call the reg'ment
'Fresh fish' and everything; but the boys come of good stock." Asked of his
own likelihood of running, Jim likewise replies in terms of group assumption. "'Well,' he replies profoundly, 'I've thought it might get too hot for Jim
Conklin in some of them scrimmages, and if a whole lot of boys started and
run, why, I s'pose I'd start and run. And if I once started to run, I'd run like the
devil and no mistake. But if everybody was a-standing and a-fighting, why,
I'd stand and fight. Be jiminey, I would. I'll bet on it'" (13). And so even the
unreliable Wilson poses some uncannily similar answers to the same question
recast shortly by Fleming as an angry challenge. "I s'pose I'll do as well as the
rest," he replies to Henry's sneering mockery. "I'm going to try like thunder."
He will do, he concludes, his "share of the fighting" (19).

So, in the analogous context of domestic virtue, we may now also read
anew the early, much-discussed scene with Henry's mother. And we see for
the first time, in passages that have too often gotten lost amidst a high interpretive symbology of potato peels and pared illusions, that the true measure
of the youth's callowness lies not, as has been generally assumed, in his disappointment at what Mrs. Fleming does not say by way of romantic valedictory.
(Having prepared a speech, he expects her to say something "about returning
with his shield or on it." With "her words," she has "destroyed his plans" [8]).
Rather, it lies in his utter incomprehension of what she does say, which is
nothing less than the whole ethos of the domestic culture, stored predictably, as in so much nineteenth-century fiction, in the hoarded wisdoms of

a woman's heart. "The Lord's will be done," his mother responds simply to his announcement that he has, against her wishes, enlisted (8). Warning him against personal vainglory, she then goes on, quite as a matter of fact, to a host of explicit directions and admonitions deeply accredited in popular domestic belief. "[A]llus be careful," she says for instance, "an' choose yer comp'ny":

> There's lot's of bad men in the army, Henry. The army makes 'em wild, and they like nothing better than the job of leading off a young feller like you, as ain't never been away from home much and has allus had a mother, an' a-learning 'em to drink and swear. Keep clear of them folks, Henry. I don't want yeh to ever do anything, Henry, that yeh would be 'shamed to let me know about. Jest think as if I was a-watchin' yeh. If yeh keep that in yer mind allus, I guess yeh'll come out about right.
>
> Ye must allus remember yer father, too, child, an' remember he never drunk a drop of licker in his life, and seldom swore a cross oath.
>
> I don't know what else to tell yeh, Henry, excepting that yeh must never do no shirking, child, on my account. If so be a time comes when yeh have to be kilt or do a mean thing, why, Henry, don't think of anything 'cept what's right, because there's many a woman has to bear up 'ginst sech things these time, and the Lord'll take keer of us all.

"Good bye, Henry," she concludes. "Watch out, and be a good boy" (8–9).

Likewise, in this context, we see why we are so drawn from the outset to the example of Jim Conklin, the domestic good man, the morally harmonious nature at ease with itself in a wise self-awareness. He eats lustily; he ruminates; he speaks a considered, homely wisdom; he "deserves" to live. And we also see why we are repelled by the example of Wilson, loud, boastful, empty. Henry's mother has warned, "Don't go a-thinkin' you can lick the hull rebel army at the start, because yeh can't. Yer just one little feller amongst a hull lot of others, and yeh've got to keep quiet an' do what they tell yeh. I know how you are Henry" (8). At the beginning Wilson proves exactly in this mold. His is the nature that does not know itself; he "deserves" to be proven a poltroon.

So, once Henry has stood fast in an initial skirmish, and then shortly, in a renewed second assault by the enemy, has committed his crucial and precipitating act of cowardice, we now see exactly the "logic" of the crucial scenes with the tattered man, with Jim Conklin in his dying, with the cheery man who leads Henry out of the night, and with Wilson again in the old unit once they have been re-united. In each case, a presumed equation between moral manhood and military duty inscribes itself in a "red badge of courage" conceived of as at once the cultural signifier *and* embodiment of the group ethos. The wound becomes the central symbolic issue in the text, then, precisely as it is granted in context a literal connection to *historical moral action* as an expression of common meaning and value.

Such, for instance, we see, is exactly the logic of the line of inquiry pursued by the tattered man in the column of wounded Henry has joined shortly after his first flight from battle. The former immediately wants to know about the youth's wound. "Where yeh hit, ol' boy," he asks "in a brotherly tone." "Where yeh hit?" (46). And later, after the deathly interlude with Jim Conklin, he returns insistently. "Ye'd better take care of yer hurt," he says. "It don't do to let sech things go. It might be inside mostly, an' them plays thunder. Where is it located?" he asks (52). It all makes for a sharp "literary" irony, that Henry's wound is literally unseen. What we now see also, however, is a new depth of cultural reference. The question stings Henry most because it is spoken by one who stands on the other side of courage and of the noble wounding. It simply never occurs to the tattered man, quite likely himself dying of wounds, that someone would join a column of wounded if he were not honorably and fairly wounded himself. Moreover, within this context exactly lies that crucial passage—indeed, the only one in the book—where the actual phrase "red badge of courage" (46) appears.

Such also exactly is the logic, we see, of extension into the scene intervening of the passion and death of Jim Conklin. Now of the tattered soldier's company in suffering brotherhood, the mortally wounded Conklin extends to Henry a bloody hand and announces immediately his innate, comradely compassion. "Where yeh been, Henry," he inquires with his first words. "I thought mebbe yeh got keeled over. There's been thunder t' pay t'-day. I was worryin about it a good deal" (47). As he begins the rite of his dying, his still-living thoughts continue to be of the need of brotherly concern. He is dreadfully afraid, he says, of being run down alone by artillery wagons. "I was allus a good friend t' yeh, wa'n't I Henry?" he beseeches. "I've allus been a pretty good feller, ain't I? An' it ain't much t' ask, is it? Jest t' pull me outer th' road? I'd do it fer you, wouldn't I, Henry?" (48). It is only when he has begun to pass to the other side, fixed his eyes at last on "the mystic place of his attentions," the final "rendezvous" (49), that he will claim solitude.

Such, finally, after Conklin's death, Henry's wanderings in the moral wilderness, and his own wounding, is the logic of the episode with the faceless man with the cheery voice. There has never been much question that his anonymity in this work—as with "the youth," "the tall soldier," "the loud soldier," etc., that Crane so carefully intercalated into his final drafts—is a major "ironic" symbology. Yet here again we now see that it is only so with the wound as the ticket, the commodity of a very particular cultural transaction, with anonymity *and* instant comradely compassion for one's discernibly enfeebled fellow quite literally bespeaking communal assumptions of the relationship between wounding and moral manhood. "Yeh seem t' be in a pretty bad way, boy?" the "cheery voice" announces out of the darkness, and the ironic "seem" leaps from the page. But already it has located its precise context of utterance in the now-familiar idea of brotherly selflessness toward the stricken. Henry grunts in assent, "thick tongued," and the voice continues. "'Well,' he said, with a round laugh, 'I'm goin' your way. Th' hull gang is goin' your way. An' I guess I kin give yeh a lift.' They began to walk like a drunken man and his friend" (62). The new friend continues to speak, confessing his own fears during the day, recalling its incredible confusions, noting a wounded officer, who, he says, "won't be talkin' so big about his reputation an' all when they go t' sawin' off his leg. Poor feller!" (62). But his chief thoughts are of his comrade Jack, killed with a curse on his lips. The voice labors on, attempting to transmute an old domestic injunction against soldierly blaspheming into the hope of peace for a fellow soul.

So, when Henry now has found his way back to his unit, the wound again becomes the instant cultural currency of his domestic re-integration, with what he knows to be the literal identification by others of its *functional* moral significance supplying the stock of his situational cunning. Sniffing out friendly emotion in the voice of a sentry who turns out to be Wilson, he quickly, Huck-like, concocts a pathetic tale of getting shot, to which Wilson responds with a touching alacrity. "What?" he cries. "Got shot? Why didn't yeh say so first? Poor ol' boy, we must—hol' on a minute; what am I doin'. I'll call Simpson" (64). Then, shortly, in an echo of the tattered soldier's overtly "ironic" query as to Henry's hidden "hurt," Wilson, examining with his fingers "the rare wound," diagnoses a grazing blow from "a ball" that seems to have "raised a queer lump jest as if some feller had lammed ye on th' head with a club" (65). But now, as the scene develops, we have already come to see that once again the fullest measure of the "ironic" character of this red badge of courage is an irony of specific cultural context, and especially now, we see, through the eyes of someone like Wilson in particular, once the "loud soldier," himself the beneficiary of a chastened and compassionate self-awareness born of the brotherhood of battle. Indeed, the real measure of the monstrosity of Henry's moral cowardice and petty egotism in these scenes depends exactly on the shifting role of the unearned wound as a visible cultural signifier for a figure such as Wilson who has clearly earned the station, to use Crane's own eloquent construction of the term at the conclusion of "The Open Boat," as an "interpreter."[9] Or, in Henry's own intuitive characterization of the figure who, for the rest of the text, will repeatedly be called "comrade" and "friend,"

The youth took note of a remarkable change in his comrade since those days of camp life upon the river bank. He seemed no more to be continually regarding the proportions of his personal prowess. He was not furious at small words that pricked his conceits. He was no more a loud young soldier. There was about him now a fine reliance. He showed a quiet belief in his purposes and his abilities. And this inward confidence evidently enabled him to be indifferent to little words of other men aimed at him.

The youth reflected. He had been used to regarding his comrade as a blatant child with an audacity grown from his inexperience, thoughtless, headstrong, jealous, and filled with a tinsel courage. A swaggering babe accustomed to strut in his own dooryard. The Youth wondered where had been born these new eyes: when his comrade had made the great discovery that there were many men who would refuse to be subjected by him. Apparently, the other had now climbed a peak of wisdom from which he could conceive himself as a very wee thing. And the youth saw that ever after it would be easier to live in his friend's neighborhood. (69)

Thus, precisely, in domestic images as old as his own mother's words in *his* old dooryard and neighborhood, Henry measures the space of manhood he has yet to cross.

Still, he browbeats Wilson, revels in his friend's clumsy solicitude, hoards up the memory of the old incriminating pre-battle confession he has made about his premonition of death. And it is exactly Henry's sense of the full uses which the wound makes available as cultural signifier that measure the exact inversion of his moral manhood against the elevation of Wilson's.

The active courage of Henry Fleming, when he gains it, comes unquestionably through a classical display of conspicuous bravery; yet in the same moment, as any number of commentators have pointed out, the motivation of that courage at virtually every point is a perplexing combination of the volitional, the instinctual, and the circumstantial. And we must make no mistake about this. The action in the book is embedded in a matrix of mechanism and external determination utterly unrelenting in its naturalistic circumstantiality. Its symbology is likewise replete with naturalistic images of monstrosity, mechanization, technologization. Nature is a cathedral sanctuary that hides a corpse, rendered definitively in a single scene in which Crane undoes a whole history of American belief, not to mention three millennia of western religion and metaphysics. Afoot in no-man's land, Henry searches nature, hurling himself from the reading of visible Providences, through the Deist argument from design, through a Romantic natural pantheism, to the dirty secret that the fundamental fact of life is the fact of death. Down to the precise notation of *real* nature, nature here is Darwinian nature, simply doing its work. It is perhaps the greatest zoom-lens scene ever written in our literature: in a text depicting from the eye of God columns of soldiers looking very like ants trundling a march across the landscape of nature, we now see through the eye of man a column of ants looking very like soldiers trundling a march along the landscape of a dead man's lip.

Similarly, the moral action of the text is a tissue of Darwinian circumstance—environmental, psychological, sociological, political, even world-historical. When Henry does initially stand in his first brief engagement, he seems to stand largely because most of the others seem to stand; and when he does run in the second, which follows almost immediately, he flees because it seems to him that all the others around him are fleeing. As noted earlier, he gains his wound while a coward in drifting, confused flight, from a coward in the full frenzy of cowardice. The subsequent construction put upon that badge of false courage by other men of true courage somehow enables him to become himself truly courageous in ways utterly unpredicted and unforeseen. In the same moment, he does so through some odd set of psychological acrobatics wherein instinct and volition seem hopelessly confused. Further, this all comes about through a series of actions themselves so hopelessly indecisive and compromised as to beggar summary: first in a repulse of the enemy resembling to him no more than "animals tossed for a death struggle in a dark pit" (79), coupled with a small advance that is merely a preface to a new collision; then in a second, longer advance that, as he and Wilson learn from an overheard officers' conversation, is intended as a suicidal stopgap and, as such, precipitates yet another desperate defensive struggle, this time with a new, advancing enemy force that seems to have blundered upon them; then, in another short withdrawal, during which we learn that Wilson's and Fleming's struggle over the regimental colors and Fleming's subsequent advancing of the emblem has earned them both personal notice for valor, but also that the prior defense-advance has fallen a hundred yards short of its objective, which is to create a diversion for another major unit attempting to seize a "real" objective; and then, finally, in yet another desperate defense against another major advance from the enemy, followed by a "real" charge which magnificently succeeds, even to Fleming's capturing of the enemy's colors,[10] but which will not matter anyhow, since it is to be part of a battle which will be "lost" by the army as a whole.

To this degree, the ironist interpreters will be correct. Man is a beast of illusion. What we can do, however, is contextualize the nature and the persistence of the illusion. Courage in its existential dimension can be measured from the baseline of courage in its cultural dimension: the specific values and beliefs for a particular soldier in a particular war in a particular context of social history.

In such a context, then, these would seem to be the major elements of a kind of composite "moral" of this story of the education of Henry Fleming about the possibility of a thing called courage amidst "the red sickness of battle" (109). First, we will find that, in a given population of soldiers in a given incident of war, the "best" in significant ways, the Jim Conklins, the ones seeming in their exemplary humanity most worthy of life, will often be taken first; and that the manner of their dying will be a ghastly animal parody of their myth-invested conceptions of spirit. It is true. A man will find his Golgotha and die like a true son of God; he will in his animal agony seek a lonely place to die like a dog. Second, we will find that the "worst," the "loud" soldiers, the ones seemingly least capable of courage and worthy of life (and who practice knuckling under in advance by turning over letters and valuables for forwarding to grief-stricken parents) become exemplary soldiers, wise, patient, compassionate, forbearing. Third, we will find that most men, given the opportunity, will turn out alternately "best" and "worst." They will prove brave in one moment, and cowardly in the next, shirking, rationalizing such behavior; yet, if spared, they may be offered the chance to try again. And, if circumstances of peer valuation permit—such as essentially, in one instance, having been not seen in an act of something that looks like cowardice and later, in another, of having been seen in an act of something that looks like courage—one may yet become, for a moment, the chief actor in what Crane called, in his immensely moving, contemporary tale, "A Mystery of Heroism;"[11] and forever afterward, one may be then remembered, for all the right and wrong reasons, to have acquitted one's self in a suspended, remarkable moment of uncanny self-transcendence. Or, as the narrator puts it, in summary and in context, of the figure he has relentlessly called "the youth," Henry Fleming becomes, at least, "a man."

And those specifics of context contained in the discourse of courage tell us that, when we see such a sentence very near the end, it must at least begin to be read, insofar as language ever makes this possible, by meaning mainly what it attempts to say: that Henry has proven commonly battleworthy by common definition, and specifically that he is as courageous as he or anyone else might expect to be; or, in some cases, not to be; or, in some other cases, again to be. Whether he is deluded or not *is* an issue and the focus throughout the narrative of a complex irony, but it is only so within this very specific context. He has simply been one of those left alive and accredited in the consensus of his fellows—and thus also in cultural memory—as having met the test. He is both an utterly self-concerned beast with illusions and a sentient, volitional being capable of visible moments of inexplicable self-transcendence, in all the mystery and wonder that attend the mighty contradiction.[12]

"He was a man," then, in context of the continuing mystery of whatever it was in that particular terrible war that still somehow made manhood possible. He was a man, that is, exactly in the context of the words men in blue and gray often used about each other: as in "braver men never shouldered a musket," from a Wisconsin private about Johnston's army before Atlanta; or, as in "we are not fighting children but men; & men worthy any foeman's steel," by a Texan after he, too, had seen the worst of it (Mitchell, 31). The tone reflected here, I submit, is quite close to the tone of Crane's assertion; and it is also the baseline where our search for the more complex tonalities of the ironic, privileged by post–Civil War perspectives, must at least begin. To be sure, it also bespeaks the gift of a precocious and moving "existential" wisdom, an understanding of and compassion for suffering humanity, that resonates throughout Crane's too-short starburst of a career. But it draws its immediate, contextual authority here, I would insist, exactly from the cultural discourse at hand. Within that particular discourse, Henry Fleming, called the "youth," undergoes a failure of courage whereby he might have been called a coward. He has not been seen, however, is not found out, and is therefore not so called. He then, given another opportunity of battle, undergoes an exhibition of courage, albeit as complex and compromised as his earlier flight, whereby he may be called something like a hero. This time, it turns out, he is seen, and he is so called, after a fashion. And it is all really just about that simple. Fleming trades momentary cowardice for momentary valor and settles for being "a jimhickey" (98). Crane works the exchange and the complex transition in the broader discourse of culture. In the beginning, as revisions in his own hand make clear, he introduces, simply, "a youthful private" (6) and "the youth" (7). In the end, after "the red sickness of battle" (109) has been passed, he eschews the epithets of both coward and hero. Rather, continuing to place courage in its contexts, and in all the contextual ironies that must prove attendant, he configures to us one last time, simply, "a man."

NOTES

1. For a detailed review of major scholarship on the focal issue of "courage," see Donald Pizer's bibliographic essay in Robert A. Rees and Earl Harbert, eds., *15 American Authors before 1900* (Madison: U of Wisconsin P, 1984), 128–84. For a re-opening of interpretive questions in light of an "authorized" edition of the text as opposed to a "sanitized" Appleton version, see Henry Binder, "*The Red Badge of Courage* Nobody Knows," in *The Red Badge of Courage* (New York: Norton, 1979), 111–58; Stephen Mailloux, "*The Red Badge of Courage* and Interpretive Conventions: Critical Response to a Maimed Text," *Studies in the Novel* 10 (1978): 48–63; and Donald Pizer, "*The Red Badge of Courage*: Text, Theme, Form," in *South Atlantic Quarterly* 84 (1985): 302–13.

Some recent historicist work has been done concerning *the author's* contexts of cultural assumption. See particularly Andrew Delbanco, "The American Stephen

Crane: The Context of *The Red Badge of Courage*," and Amy Kaplan, "The Spectacle of War in Crane's Revision of History," in *New Essays on The Red Badge of Courage*, ed. Lee Clark Mitchell (New York: Cambridge UP, 1986), 49–76 and 77–108. See also Robert Shulman, "*The Red Badge* and Social Violence: Crane's Myth of His America," in *Canadian Review of American Studies* 12.1 (1981): 1–19. Of these, Delbanco's comes closest to my own point of address in suggesting Crane's attempt to connect the experience of the war at once with the cultural values of its participants *and* with his own cultural perspective of the 1890s. "Stephen Crane wrote *The Red Badge*," says Delbanco, "out of and about a crisis of faith—both about God and about God's instrument, the American nation. He wrote it, furthermore, with a sense of disorientation in which the idea of purposeful sacrifice seemed irrecoverable. His fiction, despite its gestures of irreverence toward naive notions of heroism, is cast in the mode of lamentation for a bygone day of moral clarity" (57).

Finally, one should also mark in this respect the notable example over the years of Edwin S. Cady's work on the text, which has been throughout character-ized by an insistent and persuasive common-sense historicism. See, for instance, the chapter devoted to *The Red Badge of Courage* in *Stephen Crane*, rev. ed. (New York: Twayne, 1980), 117–44.

2. For Crane's indebtedness to *Battles and Leaders of the Civil War*, see, for instance, Howard R. Hungerford, "That Was at Chancellorsville," *American Litera-ture* 34 (1963): 520–31. For Crane's reliance on anecdotal authority, see Thomas F. O'Donnell, "John B. Van Petten: Stephen Crane's History Teacher," *American Lit-erature* 27 (1955): 196–202. For the possible influence of Civil War combat fiction, see H. T. Webster, "Wilbur F. Hinman's *Corporal Si Klegg* and Stephen Crane's *The Red Badge of Courage*," *American Literature* 11 (1939): 285–93; Thomas O'Donnell, "De Forest, Van Petten, and Stephen Crane," *American Literature* 27 (1956): 578–80; and Eric Solomon, "Another Analogue for *The Red Badge of Courage*," *Nineteenth-Century Fiction* 13 (1958): 63–67. For Crane's research into non-fictional accounts, see Stanley Wertheim, "*The Red Badge of Courage* and Personal Narratives of the Civil War," *American Literary Realism* 6 (1973): 61–65.

3. Gerald F. Lindermann, *Embattled Courage: The Experience of Combat in the American Civil War* (New York: Free Press, 1987); Reid Mitchell, *Civil War Soldiers: Their Expectations and Their Experiences* (New York: Viking, 1988). Subsequent ref-erences are parenthetical in the text.

4. Stephen Crane, *The Red Badge of Courage* (New York: Norton, 1976). Sub-sequent references are parenthetical in the text.

5. For a demonstration of the persistence of such attitudes, one may note that, in our current army, only an enlisted person may qualify for a "good conduct" medal, awarded for exactly what its name implies. For officers, apparently, such behavior continues to be assumed routine.

6. As Cady has pointed out, we should probably be warned against this in large degree on the basis of internal evidence. The title's "source," he finds, for all the efforts of allusionists to search elsewhere, really does seem to lie within the text, and situated as a localized expression of romantic symbolism within in the decidedly unironic mind of Henry Fleming, the truest believer (118).

7. Here, Mitchell can remind us instructively of one of the greatest "disil-lusionments" of the war: that an anonymous death was decidedly inglorious (60). And to extend such a logic, it can be argued, I think, that in "The Veteran," the subsequent tale so frequently adduced to inform discussions of moral manhood in

the novel, the grown-up Henry Fleming achieves exactly the noble death the youth imagines as he is spectacularly swallowed up in a burning barn for the sake of suffering fellow creatures. Stephen Crane, *Tales of War*, ed. Fredson Bowers (Charlottesville: UP of Virginia, 1970), 82–86.

8. In fact, one might propose that such a question would be more likely for one who had not been in a war. See, for example, the current example of inverse "Viet Guilt" suggested by Christopher Buckley as being felt by civilians like himself who avoided combat. *Esquire* 100 (September 1983): 68–72. From my own experience in that war, at least, although not even remotely "historical" in the sense of the data compiled by Lindermann or Mitchell, I would submit in contrast that a soldier faced with imminent combat may think about the matter of courage, but that he is far more likely to worry about death or wounds.

9. Stephen Crane, *Tales of Adventure*, ed. Fredson Bowers (Charlottesville: UP of Virginia, 1970), 68–92.

10. And lest we fall along the way into Stallmanesque rhapsodizing on the symbology of flag-advancing and flag-capturing—of Henry's wrenching his own unit emblem in concert and then contest with Wilson from a dying color bearer in blue and then wresting yet another, this time Confederate, from a dying "other" in gray—this too turns out, as Mitchell shows us decisively, to be heavily compromised by a specific logic of context. For Civil War soldiers, it was simply a cultural fact, he shows, that a unit flag, often fashioned "by the women of the community," was in and of itself accorded a preternatural *domestic* importance as a cultural signifier. "The flag was the physical tie between the homelife they had left and fought for," he writes, "and the war into which they were plunged. In Civil War battles, the importance of advancing one's flag and defending it from capture—and, conversely, capturing enemy flags—indicates a devotion to flags far beyond what military rationality might seem to demand" (19–20).

11. Stephen Crane, *Tales of War* (Charlottesville: UP of Virginia, 1970), 48–56.

12. Again, if we read historically, Crane tells us as much in terms both of individual and of collective possibility, exactly in the midst of historical action—here in simply one more charge among a series of advances and retreats to be concluded in a local victory eventually swallowed up in a larger defeat—exactly in *context* of experience already somehow rendered across the years into the gaze of cultural memory:

> The men, pitching forward insanely, had burst into cheerings, moblike and barbaric, but tuned in strange keys that can arouse the dullard and the stoic. It made a mad enthusiasm that, it seemed, would be incapable of checking itself before granite and brass. There was the delirium that encounters despair and death, and is heedless and blind to the odds. It is a temporary but sublime absence of selfishness. And because it was of this order was the reason, perhaps, why the youth wondered, afterward, what reasons he could have had for being there. (87)

Compare, now, in Mitchell's text, the personal report from a Union combatant at Gettysburg:

Charge we did drove the foe like chaff before the wind. Strange it does seem to be these men that a few moments before was driving our Men Now threw Down their arms & begged for mercy at our hands they said they could not stand our fire Strange too, our men that A Short time before seemed to be almost Dead was now as full of life and vigor as men could be As for myself, I never felt better then I did when making that grand charge. (80)

VERNER D. MITCHELL

Reading *"Race"* and *"Gender"* in
Crane's The Red Badge of Courage

T aking my cue primarily from Nobel Laureate Toni Morrison's "Unspeakable Things Unspoken: The Afro-American Presence in American Literature" (1989) and *Playing in the Dark: Whiteness and the Literary Imagination* (1993), I want to offer, in this brief paper, what I trust will be a relatively new look at Stephen Crane's classic civil war novel, *The Red Badge of Courage*. In a 1992 review of Melville scholarship, critic Andrew Delbanco writes that Morrison's "Unspeakable Things Unspoken"[1] "opens new entrances into Melville in ways that earlier estimable works . . . had not quite managed to do. It will be a long time," he adds, "before these entrances are closed."[2] Morrison's critical work offers, I would contend, an equally fortuitous opening into Crane. For with the exception of criticism on *George's Mother* and *Maggie*, and on "The Monster," signs of "gender and "race" in Crane's fiction have gone largely uninterrogated—or, in Morrison's language, they have been unspeakable and unspoken. The foregrounding of constructions of "gender" and "race" therefore promises to offer new openings into *The Red Badge* and, perhaps more importantly, suggests that in his most successful work Crane challenges, and in some instances subverts categories which controlled much of nineteenth-century Euro-American thought.

Ralph Ellison in his 1986 work *Going to the Territory* notes perceptively that *The Red Badge of Courage* "is about the Civil War, but only one black

From *CLA Journal* 40, no. 1 (September 1996) 60–71. Copyright © 1996 by the College Language Association.

person appears, and then only briefly."[3] After zooming in on his character, however, Ellison, like most other critics, seems at a loss concerning exactly what to make of the novel's unnamed black man. That they would have such difficulty is not at all surprising, given that the black man drops in (seemingly out of nowhere) for all of two sentences, and then he disappears, just as abruptly, never to be heard from again. The novel's opening scene shows Jim Conklin rushing back from washing a shirt in order to broadcast excitedly, though erroneously, that the regiment will attack the following day. "To his attentive audience," reports the narrator, Conklin

> drew a loud and elaborate plan of a very brilliant campaign. When he had finished, the blue-clothed men scattered into small arguing groups between the rows of squat brown huts. A negro [sic] teamster who had been dancing upon a cracker box with the hilarious encouragement of two-score soldiers was deserted. He sat mournfully down.[4]

I want to linger, for just a moment, on the variously dancing and mournful character.

At its most basic level, the description is simply one of a black man dancing, in typical minstrel fashion, so as to entertain a group of white men.[5] This dancing black man and his amused audience, especially with the rows of "squat brown huts" as backdrop, would appear to be more at home in postbellum, romanticized defenses of slavery. Even so, the three-sentence side show, when situated within the era's typical portraits of African Americans, would not be particularly noteworthy were it not for the fact, as Ralph Ellison reminds us, that Crane's is a novel of the Civil War. Yet precisely because the American Civil War is the novel's subject,[6] this fleeting portrait of black–white interaction actually drives to the very heart of *The Red Badge*. Why do Henry and his colleagues enlist? Why are they fighting, risking and all too often losing their lives? On this crucial point, even the characters themselves remain unclear. By means of their "hilarious encouragement" of the teamster and even more so their rudely abrupt departure, they do signal, however, that for them their black colleague is of little, if any, consequence. As a result, although we cannot determine exactly why they are fighting, we can see rather clearly that abolition, Negro freedom, and black uplift are far from the top of their agenda.

Amy Kaplan offers a more sympathetic reading In a probing, subtly-nuanced analysis, she maintains that in an effort to map new arenas for warfare and for imaginative literature, Crane divorces both the Civil War from its historical context and his novel from generic narrative conventions.[7] Hence the opening scene, rather than an endorsement, is actually a rejection of minstrelsy. She explains that "[i]n the 1880s, tales of chivalric exploits . . . superseded the older narrative of emancipation." Crane, therefore, by divorcing his own narrative from these "former stories about freeing the slaves" actually "calls attention to the process whereby the history of emancipation has been reduced to a form of entertainment." The novel's sympathy, then, in Kaplan's view, rests not with the laughing two-score soldiers, but with the "deserted" teamster who "sits 'mournfully down' to lament his loss of an audience and his own passing as a figure for the subject of emancipation."[8]

Kaplan's reading, while not altogether convincing, is especially helpful to the extent that it locates the teamster center stage, rescuing him, at last, from the textual and critical margins. In so doing, she retards what Morrison has referred to as long-standing acts of "willful critical blindness."[9] Nonetheless, any number of critics continue to argue, as does Daniel Aaron, that "Crane's soldiers . . . have no antecedents to speak of, no politics, no prejudices. Negroes and Lincoln and hospitals and prisons," he maintains, "are not to be found in Crane's theater; these and other matters were irrelevant to his main concern—the nature of war and what happens to people who engage in it."[10] Here we are told that Crane focuses on people and that Negroes and other similar irrelevances are not to be found in his theater. Such readings so marginalize the novel's black man (and his interests) that he is all but pushed out of *The Red Badge* and rendered invisible. In contrast, the novel's young protagonist, Private Henry Fleming, finds it much more difficult to escape such matters as politics and prejudices, hospitals and Negroes.

Since my own analysis thus far has focused on how the laughing soldiers view the teamster, I also think it important, like Kaplan, to examine how he views them and even more importantly, how he views himself. As the twoscore soldiers depart, does the teamster actually sit mournfully down to lament his passing as a figure for the subject of emancipation, or does he merely lament his loss of an audience? If the latter is true, and I suspect that it is, then the teamster sees himself (or at least the novel would have us believe that he sees himself) as a subservient appendage to a group of other men. Rather than utter a healthy sigh of relief at their departure, he apparently prefers that they remain and continue their "hilarious encouragement." He thus measures his self-worth, as Du Bois would phrase it, through the eyes of those who "look on in amused contempt."[11] Notice, too, that the only visible role that the novel permits him is as entertainer for the dominant culture and according to the dominant culture's limited expectations. As a result, in this, the novel's opening scene, Crane has masterfully constructed a rigid, racialized hierarchy, one which dates back in American literature at least to Jefferson's *Notes on the State of Virginia* (1787). Simply put, Crane's dancing black man boosts the white soldiers' egos and their sense of self-worth, and in so doing he serves as a convenient device for cementing both his and their God-ordained place on the Great Racial Chain of Being.

As we flip to page two, the teamster is figuratively buried, never to be heard from again. In his place surfaces a more abstract, less concrete figuration of darkness, one which Morrison in a somewhat different context has labeled a "disrupting darkness."[12] What we might term "the great unseen presence in the text," therefore, persists. Chapter 16, for example, finds Henry reveling in his recently received red badge of courage. The narrator notes, somewhat derisively, that Henry "had performed his mistakes in the dark, so he was still a man. Indeed," he continues, "when he remembered his fortunes of yesterday, and looked at these from a distance he began to see something fine there. He had license to be pompous and veteran-like" (79). Here darkness is presented as a positive and perhaps even benevolent force. In keeping concealed the fact that Henry's wound, his bandage of courage, occurred as a consequence of his throwing down his rifle and running "like a rabbit" (35), the darkness enables, his manhood to remain intact. Of course the darkness does not blind Henry to the circumstances of his wound nor, by extension, to the substance of what he considers his "manhood." Hence in this scene we can begin to understand his ambivalence toward darkness, or what I prefer to call his love–hate relationship with blackness.

In the chapter's succeeding paragraphs, Henry undertakes a more sustained meditation on blackness. He is now a man of experience, an authentic hero, and he accordingly struts about and looks with scorn upon lesser men. To capture the passage's essence, I need quote at length:

> Some poets ... had wandered in paths of pain and they had made pictures of the black landscape that others might enjoy it with them. He had, at that time, been sure that their wise, contemplating spirits had been in sympathy with him, had shed tears from the clouds. ...
>
> But he was now, in a measure, a successful man and he could no longer tolerate in himself a spirit of fellowship with poets. He abandoned them. Their songs about black landscapes were of no importance to him since his new eyes said that his landscape was not black. People who called landscapes black were idiots. He achieved a mighty scorn for such a snivelling race. (80)

The antecedent of "snivelling race," I would argue, is intentionally vague. Does "snivelling race," for instance, refer to the poet race or, just as likely, to the black race? Here, as elsewhere throughout the novel, the passage is sufficiently complex to accommodate multiple readings. What seems indisputable, however, and what for me is the more salient point, is that within the passage, "blackness" takes on for Henry (as it does throughout Western civilization) a clear and unrelentingly negative connotation. What is equally clear is that the scene's biting irony renders Henry's judgment vain at worst and naive at best. Therefore, where the portrait of the teamster reinforces myopic conceptions of blackness and whiteness, Henry's ironized "scorn for such a snivelling race" challenges, perhaps unintentionally, all such constructions.

A later meeting between Henry and two members of the army's elite brings the novel's evolving depiction of "race" into even sharper focus. In chapter 19, Henry and another "foot-soldier" happen to overhear two officers insulting their regiment, the 304th. In this scene, we as readers are positioned with the foot soldiers, and we accordingly must similarly stand back and listen, unseen, and afterwards interpret the officers' conversation:

> The officer who rode like a cow-boy reflected for an instant. "Well," he said, "I had to order in th' 12th to help th' 76th an' I haven't really got any. But there's th' 304th. They fight like a lot 'a mule-drivers. I can spare them best of any." The youth and his friend exchanged glances of astonishment. The general spoke sharply. "Get 'em ready then. . . ." As the other officer tossed his fingers toward his cap and, wheeling his horse, started away, the general called out to him in a sober voice: "I don't believe many of your mule-drivers will get back." (92–93)

The uncomplimentary label "mule-drivers" bridges the color divide by figuratively linking Henry and his regimental brothers to the Negro teamster, who is literally a mule-driver. Once again, Morrison aids our interpretation. She writes in *Sula* of "old women who worried about such things as bad blood mixtures and knew that the origins of a mule and a mulatto were one and the same."[13] Indeed, an attentive examination of Henry's "glance of astonishment" reveals that he understands that which Morrison's old women understand, and like them he fears being collapsed into an arena of mules and other "mixed" beings, and thus placed on the bottom rung of humankind's evolutionary ladder. To be sure, Henry's gender and race set him above and apart from Morrison's old women. His race and phenotype do the same vis-à-vis the Negro teamster/mule-driver. Yet viewed through the general's eyes, they are all, at bottom, much the same. Crane's narrator reports that in listening to the officers "the most startling thing [for Henry] was to learn suddenly that he was very insignificant" (93). Henry certainly realizes, then, that the officers see him as mere cannon fodder, as one whose class renders him little better than Negroes and mules and such.

At first glance, Henry's romanticized encounter with a "dark girl," just prior to his leaving for the war, seems to further problematize stereotypic notions of blackness and whiteness. So, too, does the opening chapter's description of Henry's mother's "brown face" (6). Before turning to Henry and his brown-faced mother, whose extended conversation will shortly bring this paper to a close, I want to comment first on his encounter with the dark girl. We certainly need not look far into the canon of American literature to find synecdochial signifiers of race, more often than not ones mapped onto and played out by means of the female body. Let me offer three specific examples. In Cooper's *The Last of the Mohicans* (1826), Alice and Cora Munro brave a gauntlet of dangers to visit their father, a British officer fighting against the French in hostile Indian territory. During the course of their journey, dark-haired Cora, whose mother is West Indian,[14] is killed; her golden-haired, blue-eyed half-sister, Alice,[15] in contrast, lives and can thus marry and propagate the race in her own image. Hawthorne's *The Blithedale Romance* (1852) makes use of a similar pattern. Zenobia, a dark-haired woman drawn to recall and mock the pioneering feminist Margaret Fuller, drowns herself after being rejected by Hollingsworth.[16] Hollingsworth chooses, instead, "fair" Priscilla, who is painted as "perfectly modest, delicate, and virginlike."[17] Moreover, in the novel's famous last sentence, the narrator discloses that he, too, prefers Priscilla: "I—I myself—was in love—with—Priscilla!"[18] Even in Alcott's *Little Women* (1868), which like *The Red Badge* is set during the Civil War, it is a dark-haired sister, Beth, who catches scarlet fever and dies.[19] And it is her sister Amy, described as "A regular snow maiden with blue eyes, and yellow hair," who lives, eventually marrying the man whom Beth had fallen in love with and giving birth to a "golden-haired" baby girl.[20] Rather than cite additional instances of what eventually became a staple in nineteenth-century American literature, suffice it to say that Henry's longing for a dark girl stands this pattern on its head. Not only does he dismiss, rather decisively, a light-haired girl, and she him, but he finds (or at least he thinks that he does) in the dark girl his potential soul mate:

> From his home, he had gone to the seminary to bid adieu to many schoolmates. They had thronged about him with wonder and admiration.... A certain lighthaired girl had made vivacious fun at his martial-spirit but there was another and darker girl whom he had gazed at steadfastly and he thought she grew demure and sad at the sight of his blue and brass. As he had walked down the path between the rows of oaks, he had turned his head and detected her at a window watching his departure. (6)

The above description of Henry desiring a dark girl rather than the unattractive, stereotypical blonde-haired beauty, challenges and arguably subverts common turn-of-the-century constructions of race and gender. Henry's relationship with his brown-faced mother, however, is less clear-cut. Henry's mother, similar to his light-haired female schoolmate, "look[s] with some contempt upon the quality of his war-ardor and patriotism" (3). When he tells her that he has decided to enlist, she replies succinctly and bluntly, "Henry, don't you be a fool" (4). The ensuing verbal give-and-take between Henry and his mother, which is at bottom little more than a duel or a gendered battle,[21] draws to a close when Henry enlists. As he views it, "he had made firm rebellion against this yellow light thrown upon the color of his ambitions" (4).

Nonetheless, a short while later Henry finds himself wishing, without reserve, that he had needed his mother's advice. In this rare moment, for him, of clear thought, the yellow light personifies safety, courage, and insight, while brass buttons and red badges are merely the unfortunate by-products of a hyper and misguided masculine ethos. Feeling sorry for himself,

> [h]e wish[es] without reserve that he was at home again, making the endless rounds, from the house to the barn, from the barn to the fields, from the fields to the barn, from the barn to the house. He remembered he had often cursed the brindle-cow and her mates, and had sometimes fung milking-stools. But from his present point of view, there was a halo of happiness about each of their heads and he would have sacrificed all the brass buttons on the continent to have been enabled to return to them. (15)

This picture of a frustrated Henry milking cows, of him in fact as a milkmaid, captures compellingly the domestic realm which he had made firm rebellion against. But now, only a short while after having charged forth to become "a man," he would all too willingly retrace his steps. Indeed, he wishes with all his heart that he could step back over that dividing line which he had erroneously come to see as separating men from women, bulls from cows.

Unfortunately, this moment of lucidity does not last. A few chapters later he is again neck-deep in dreams of heroism and valor, of bloody battles and brass buttons. To cite one brief instance, toward the end of chapter sixteen he pictures himself back home

> in a room of warm tints telling tales to listeners. . . . He saw his gaping audience picturing him as the central figure in blazing

scenes. And he imagined the consternation and the ejaculations of his mother and the young lady at the seminary as they drank his recitals. Their vague feminine formula for beloved ones doing brave deeds on the field of battle without risk of life, would be destroyed. (82)

Of course the irony here is too apparent to be missed. This vague feminine formula for beloved ones doing brave deeds on the field of battle which Henry details is neither his mother's nor his female classmate's. Instead, Henry is actually describing his own mistaken masculine formula, and it is the two women who have tried valiantly, though unsuccessful, to destroy it. Recall that when young Henry initially boasts of his forthcoming martial exploits, his mother cries out, in disgust, "Henry, don't . . . be a fool." Likewise, to the extent that the young woman at the seminary grows demure and sad at his departure, she, too, in all likelihood sees what he even by novel's end cannot see. The novel, therefore, in this and similar scenes, forcefully exposes and explodes what I earlier labeled Henry's misguided masculine ethos.

Hence for Henry to recognize and afterwards construct a more wholesome definition of manhood, he must first embrace his mother's teachings and thus collapse his flawed nations of the feminine and the masculine. No less important, constructing a healthier definition of personhood requires that he also move beyond hierarchical, dichotomous notions of race. Likely the novel's great message, then, for Henry and his critics alike, is that they look to the margins: to his dark-skinned potential lover, his African-American brother in arms, and his wise, though generally ignored, brown-faced mother.

Notes

Author's note: I wish to thank Professors Donald B. Gibson and John Clendenning for their help with this essay.

1. See Toni Morrison, "Unspeakable Things Unspoken: The Afro-American Presence in American Literature," *Michigan Quarterly Review* 28.1 (Winter 1989): 1–34.

2. Andrew Delbanco, "Melville in the '80's," *American Literary History* 4.4 (Winter 1992): 722.

3. Ralph Ellison, *Going to the Territory* (New York: Vintage, 1987) 237.

4. Stephen Crane, *The Red Badge of Courage* (1895; New York: Avon, 1982) 1. Hereafter cited parenthetically in the text by page reference only.

5. For an excellent analysis of minstrelsy, see Eric Lott, *Love and Theft: Blackface Minstrelsy and the American Working Class* (New York: Oxford UP, 1993).

6. The novel's full title is *The Red Badge of Courage: An Episode of the American Civil War*.

7. Amy Kaplan, "The Spectacle of War in Crane's Revision of History," in *New Essays on The Red Badge of Courage*, ed. Lee Clark Mitchell (New York: Cambridge UP, 1986) 78.

8. Kaplan 85.

9. Toni Morrison, *Playing in the Dark: Whiteness and the Literary Imagination* (New York: Vintage, 1993) 18.

10. Daniel Aaron, *The Unwritten War* (Madison, U of Wisconsin P, 1987) 214–15.

11. W. E. B. Du Bois, *The Souls of Black Folk* (1903; New York: Vintage, 1990) 8.

12. Morrison 91.

13. Toni Morrison, *Sula* (New York: Plume, 1973) 52.

14. James Fenimore Cooper, *The Last of the Mohicans* (1826; New York: Signet, 1980) 118, 187.

15. Cooper 20.

16. Nathaniel Hawthorne, *The Blithedale Romance* (1852; New York: Oxford UP, 1991) 15, 47.

17. Hawthorne 77.

18. Hawthorne 274; emphasis Hawthorne's.

19. Louisa May Alcott, *Little Women* (1868; New York: Penguin, 1989) 177, 183, 419.

20. Alcott 4, 489.

21. Chapter two contains another gendered battle. In this contest, the male is again found lacking and a young, pink-cheeked female proves his superior. A rather fat soldier attempted to pilfer a horse from a dooryard, He planned to load his knapsack upon it. He was escaping with his prize when a young girl rushed from the house and grabbed the animal's mane. There followed a wrangle. The young girl, with pink cheeks and shining eyes, stood like a dauntless statue. . . . The regiment rejoiced at his downfall. Loud and vociferous congratulations were showered upon the maiden, who stood panting and regarding the troops with defiance" (14).

MAX WESTBROOK

The Progress of Henry Fleming:
Stephen Crane's The Red Badge of Courage

Egocentricity, especially when it leads to rationalizations away from personal responsibility, is the primary target of Stephen Crane's characteristic irony.[1] In *The Red Badge of Courage*, for example, instead of privileging Henry Fleming's rationalizations and contradictions as proof of determinism, Crane exposes and judges the youth's foolish dreams and selfish dishonesty, relenting only when Fleming is finally able "to more closely comprehend himself and circumstance" (Levenson 210).

Numerous scenes and specific images, however, are so striking that *The Red Badge* has been read as both episodic and allegorical.[2] The problem is Crane's deceptive style. When writing dialogue, Crane lets his characters speak for themselves, but their private thoughts are devoiced and reported in the narrator's ironically judgmental voice. When a character's thinking meets with the narrator's approval—a rare occurrence for Henry Fleming—the irony is dropped, and the language is flat, as in the simple statement, "He was a man" (212).

The ironic narrative voice consistently employs detachment, a long-range viewpoint, to reveal discrete moments in the egocentric imagination of a terrified youth. Fleming confronts the whole world from the restrictive and totally subjective viewpoint of a single moment. When his fleeting reflections change, the world according to Henry Fleming also changes. *The Red Badge* is thus a diachronic telling of Fleming's synchronic distortions and rationalizations.

From *The CEA Critic* 61, nos. 2–3 (Winter and Spring/Summer 1999): 71–82. Copyright © 1999 by the College English Association.

By decoding Crane's narrative voice, we can see that *The Red Badge* is neither allegorical nor episodic. If images and scenes are then read in their relevant contexts and the continuity of the narrative is recognized, the novel seems more concrete than allegorical and the language unified rather than disconnected.

In the last chapter, for example, Crane says that Fleming "had been to *touch the great death*, and found that, after all, it was but the great death" (212; emphasis added). Read as a discrete image, the comment seems absurd. Neither a naive and freshly declared hero enjoying sudden maturation nor a fool suffering from new-found illusions would face his unmistakable demise and say, "Never mind; it's only death."

The image, however, is the climax of a series of events and insights used to describe Fleming's various reactions as he is forced to confront the idea of his own death. Early in the novel, before Fleming has seen combat, he personifies death and imagines himself as a selected and personal target: He "glared about him, expecting to see the stealthy approach of his death" (102). That afternoon, Fleming indulges in a fantasy of self-pity: He decides to die and "go to some place where he would be understood" (105).

When he comes upon the dead man in the forest chapel, he imagines death as a grotesque, magical ogre. He is afraid that if he turns his back, "the body might spring up and stealthily pursue him." In spite of his fear, he feels an urge "to *touch the corpse*," but then he runs away because he is afraid "some strange voice would come *from the dead throat* and squawk after him in horrible menaces" (127; emphasis added). Coming upon "four or five corpses keeping mournful company," Fleming is afraid "that one of the swollen forms would rise and tell him to begone" (129). Basing his conclusions about reality on fragmented moments has caused the youth to imagine a world filled with the trappings of a Gothic novel.

Finding that death is "but the great death" does not suggest that Fleming has come to a superficial evasion of an awesome reality. The suggestion, rather, is that he "shuddered profoundly" at the thought of touching death—that is, at the thought of an actual, tactile experience of death as distinguished from the "neat plan" (106) of a merely imagined death or the nightmarish death pictured by his fear. At the end of the novel, as we have seen, he has "been to touch the great death." He has progressed from synchronic illusions—death is a corporeal fiend pursuing him personally, death is a place where he will be understood, dead bodies will berate or chase him—to a diachronic understanding of death as an awesome force ("the great death") that is neither a supernatural horror nor a comforter conscious of and interested in an individual named Henry Fleming.

Fleming's growth from "a babe" (100) or "beast" (113) to "a man" (212) suggests considerable progress toward maturity, but *The Red Badge* is more concerned with a revolving process than with closure in the story of Henry Fleming. The youth also develops "an attitude of manfulness" even before he has done anything heroic—and merely because he "performed his mistakes in the dark" (165), and the successful lie about his "red badge of courage" (133) leads him to conclude that he is "still a man" and has "a license to be pompous and veteranlike" (165). In the final passages, Fleming has progressed, but he is only two days older, still young enough to be silent about his flight from combat. Crane, a realist, knew it would be psychologically convincing to have Fleming confess his initial cowardice (in "The Veteran") only when he had more firmly proved himself in combat and after many years had passed.

Crane's diachronic vision of an initiation story marked by backsliding and contradictions includes Wilson, the "loud" soldier. At first, Fleming thinks Wilson is "a blatant child," a "swaggering babe" (161); yet, after the first day of fighting, Wilson has apparently "climbed a peak of wisdom from which he could perceive himself as a very wee thing" (161), a foreshadowing of Fleming's realization that he is "very insignificant" (179).

But Wilson is no more perfect after climbing his "peak of wisdom" than Fleming is predicted to be at the end of the novel. Shortly after Fleming grabs the flag away from Wilson and the regiment retreats, Wilson comes to his friend and repeats the gloomy prophecy he had made earlier when he was still called the loud soldier: "Well, Henry, I guess this is good-by-John." Fleming tells him to "shut up" (191).

When the general berates the colonel for retreating, Wilson begins to complain in a now uncharacteristic petulance: The general "must think we went out there an' played marbles." This time it is Fleming who, for the moment, takes on the role of the mature soldier: "Oh well . . . , he probably didn't see nothing of it at all . . ." (197). When Wilson continues his immature complaint and threatens to "stay behind [the] next time" the regiment charges, he is not speaking from a "peak of wisdom." Then Fleming, whose moment of maturity is no more absolute than Wilson's "peak of wisdom," gets caught up in his friend's jawing and breaks out with "sudden exasperation," calling the general a "lunkhead" (197). Progress, in Crane's diachronic world, includes steps forward, steps backward, societal pressures, harsh and often cruel circumstances, and emotional extremes that are appropriate for soldiers in their first two days of combat.

Along the way, motive—what a person wills toward—is more important to character development than what grade that person might earn on some single-standard scale of moral performance. In his admirable *The Pluralistic*

Philosophy of Stephen Crane, Patrick Dooley writes, "Crane rejects [Immanuel Kant's] categorical imperatives that command exceptionless obedience to universal maxims" (94). Crane was no Kantian, but his credo of "personal honesty" (Wertheim and Sorrentino 195)—doing the best one can with what one has been given—is a tough-minded newspaper reporter's version of Kant's four formulations of his categorical imperative. Because it requires no specific code of behavior and emphasizes motives rather than predetermined rules, the categorical imperative can be applied universally. Exceptions are not the issue, because the categorical imperative recognizes the necessity of granting individual circumstances *before* an ethical judgment can be made. A major difference between Crane and Kant is that Crane would grant far more power to environment than would the pristine and sheltered Kant. Both, however, believed that human beings have an ethical responsibility to seek to bring about the good with whatever ability they have to see it and with whatever ability they have to enact it.

Crane's emphasis on will in *The Red Badge* is characteristic of his writings. Maggie Johnson, for example, does the best she can with what she has been given. Maggie does not "feel like a bad woman. To her knowledge, she had never seen any better" (53), and thus she is not subjected to Crane's satire. Her brother Jimmie, by contrast, rejects the ethical obligations he does have an opportunity to see, and he rejects them out of a bad will: "Two women in different parts of the city . . . caused him *considerable annoyance* by breaking forth, simultaneously, at fateful intervals, into wailings about marriage and support and infants" (23; emphasis added). Jimmie's devoiced suffering is reported in the same ironic voice used to show Fleming's egocentricity. Maggie and Jimmie's mother, Mary Johnson, is such an extreme example of personal dishonesty that she could be called a caricature.

Henry Fleming's motives, as often noted, are flawed from the very beginning. He enlists because of a selfish desire for newspaper glory and romantic adulation. He is not interested in patriotism or civil rights. In his reflections, he apologizes for the war's lack of tales that are "distinctly Homeric" but still yearns to enlist because "there seemed to be much glory in them." He has read newspaper stories of the war, and his "busy mind ha[s] drawn for him large pictures extravagant in color, lurid with breathless deeds" (83). He believes that a dark-haired young girl "grew demur and sad at sight of his blue and brass" (86).

Mrs. Fleming, however, looks "with some contempt upon the quality of his war ardor and patriotism" (83). She thinks it would be more sensible for him to stay on the farm than join the army. Basically, "on her side, was *his* belief that *her ethical motive* in the argument was impregnable" (84; emphasis added). Finally, "however, he had made firm rebellion against this yellow light thrown upon the color of his ambitions" (84). Leaving to join the army, Fleming looks back and sees his mother "kneeling among the potato parings" and crying: "He bowed his head and went on, feeling suddenly *ashamed of his purposes*" (85; emphasis added).

In the last chapter, the statement that Fleming has "rid himself of the red sickness of battle" (212) needs to be read in the context of his awareness of and responsibility for his selfish "ambitions," his dreams of Greek heroics that would be no more. His education includes the realization that heroism in war may be a "red sickness" rather than something grand and glorious. In *The Red Badge*, achieving heroism in the face of arbitrary death is a cruel process, a dangerous way to purge one's self of egocentric dreams of glory.[3]

Images such as the following—referring sometimes to Fleming, sometimes to the regiment[4]—suggest what drives people to fight in a war: "hate" (174); "an insane soldier" (182); "a madman" (186); the "insane fever of haste," "mob of blue men ... grown suddenly wild with an enthusiasm of unselfishness," "sublime recklessness" (204); "state of frenzy," "the daring spirit of a savage, religion-mad," "wild battle madness" (205); "mad horse," "beaks and claws" (206); and "mad cry of exultation" (207). Even Wilson, when he sees a wounded Confederate flag bearer, leaps for "the flag as a panther at prey." As the flag bearer dies, Wilson grabs the emblem "with a mad cry of exultation" (207).

Having experienced "battle madness," Fleming turns, finally, with "a lover's thirst to images of tranquil skies, fresh meadows, cool brooks—an existence of soft and eternal peace" (212). If Crane is describing a newly created illusion, *The Red Badge* is a case-study of a psychopath; but I think a better reading comes from responding to Crane's invitation to read the last chapter in terms of what has gone before: "The sultry nightmare was in the past. He had been an animal blistered and sweating in the heat and pain of war" (212). Fleming's ambitions for glory and his fear of disgrace have led him to behave like "an animal," but now he is thinking like a "lover"—that is, a human being. Images of "monsters" and dead men who "squawk" have been replaced by images of nature and peace.

Jim Conklin, the "tall" soldier, does not survive long enough to undergo a significant change, but his death is an integral chapter in the story of Fleming's roundabout progress from rationalizations toward maturity. The critical debate about the tall soldier may be divided, roughly, into two camps: first, critics who believe that Conklin is a Christ figure, the "red wafer" is a Christian symbol, and Fleming, at the end of the novel, is redeemed; second, critics who believe that Conklin is not a Christ figure and that Fleming's final achievement is merely a new illusion, or else that the novel suffers from a badly flawed ending.[5]

I believe that this debate is based on a false dichotomy. Clearly, the novel asks the reader to associate Conklin with Christ—the initials J. C., the "bloody hands" (136), the wound in the side (137) if the specific language is ignored, and the words suggesting that Conklin's death is a ritualistic sacrifice: "solemn ceremony," "something ritelike," "rendezvous" (136), "ceremony at the place of meeting" (137).

Evidence for rejecting the Christ analogy is equally clear however: the image of an "animal" in Conklin's chest "kicking and tumbling furiously to be free" (136); the description of a tremor that causes the dying Conklin to dance a "hideous hornpipe," his arms beating "wildly" in "implike enthusiasm" (137); and finally the description of his dead, "pastelike face" with "teeth" showing "in a laugh" (137).

Since standard associations with Christ and sharp variations from the Christ story both appear in the novel, why should we opt for one and deny the other? Crane's reason for including ambiguous signals, I think, is indicated by his most fundamental change in the traditional Christ story: Jim Conklin is not in the service of the Christian God. He is "a devotee of a mad religion, blood-sucking, muscle-wrenching, bone-crushing" (136)—namely, the god of war. Simply, Crane has said to the reader: You know the story of Jesus Christ and the meaning of his sacrifice to the biblical God; this is the story of Jim Conklin and the meaning (or lack of meaning) of his sacrifice to the god of war.

Once again, Crane is thinking both/and, not either/or. As we see in Chapter 3, Conklin is a good soldier. He does spread rumors, argue heatedly, and get in a fistfight, but his emotional explosions are a sign of pride and overly excited anticipation, not of disobedience. When the wisdom of the regiment's leadership is questioned, the tall soldier quietly demonstrates his loyalty. Fleming, for example, complains about being ordered to move out as soon as the men have finished "erecting tiny hills" (103) for protection. Conklin, "with calm faith," immediately begins "a heavy explanation, although he had been compelled to leave a little protection of stones and dirt to which he had devoted much care and skill" (104).

Fleming next complains about being "marched from place to place with apparent aimlessness," and Conklin, now dubbed "the philosophical tall soldier," again tries to defend the orders of the commanding officers: "Oh, I suppose we must go reconnoitering around the country jest to keep 'em from getting too close, or to develop 'em, or something" (104).

Coming off poorly in his attempt to hush the complaining loud soldier, Conklin eats "as if taking poison in despair" but then becomes peaceful, as his "spirit" seems "to be communing with the viands" (105). The good soldier dines—and does so with ecstasy—at the convenience of the army. In addition, he marches and works as ordered and without whining or complaining: "He accepted new environment and circumstance with great coolness, eating from his haversack at every opportunity. On the march he went along with the stride of a hunter, objecting to neither gait nor distance" (105).

Crane's good soldier, however, serves a bloodthirsty god. Before the regiment has seen combat, the men go forward "to look at war, the red animal—war, the blood-swollen god" (103). As the second attack begins, Crane writes, the "slaves toiling in the temple of this god began to feel rebellion at his harsh tasks" (118). Such imagery, of course, represents the exaggerated imaginations of soldiers in their first day of combat, but Conklin's devotion to the god of war results in his dying with a wound in his side that "looked as if it had been chewed by wolves" (137). The beginning of death for the "tattered man" is a pitiful sight, and Crane's descriptions of generalized death and of specific bodies constitute a vivid critique of the horrors of war.[6] In *The Red Badge*, both flight and courage seem dehumanizing, at least at the moment of happening.

Nonetheless, the novel expresses an admiration for courage in combat, and we know that Crane did admire bravery.[7] Wildly charging forward into enemy fire has the beneficial effect on Fleming and on the regiment in general of earning them, afterward, the word "man" instead of "animal" or "madman," but that progress—ongoing or temporary—is possible only for those lucky enough to survive. To see the ideological backdrop of Crane's ambiguous attitudes toward war, toward Conklin, and toward the question of Fleming's progress, it is helpful to look at the infamous "red wafer" image (137), in both its immediate and structural contexts.

Henry Fleming is a youth, a farm boy with an imagination that instantly paints glorious dreams of heroism and garish portraits of death. He is isolated because of his terror of war and his internal debate between the glory he desires and the cowardice he fears. The youth feels that his spastic stand against the first charge should have been his allotment of horror, but during the more consciously observed second charge, he bolts. Then comes a series of unsuccessful rationalizations. There seems to be no alleviation for the guilt-ridden and terrified youth, but then he finds Jim Conklin stalking precariously among the wounded. Finally, Fleming has found relief for his agony. Here is something honorable he can do: He can help his wounded friend. But then Conklin refuses help and, driven by a mysterious compulsion, runs to his death. With "sudden, livid rage" (137), Fleming shakes his fist at the cause of his misery—the battlefield, the war—as if to deliver a sharp speech of protest against the injustice of forces that oppress him.

Crane then draws a parallel between the immediate scene he has painted and the ongoing story he is telling: "The red sun was pasted in the sky like a wafer" (137). The sky is sealed off as an envelope is sealed off with a wax wafer.[8] The universe, the ultimate—whatever the final power may be—does not condescend to answer the protests of mere human beings. Egocentric demands for answers or personal attention from the universe are met with silence.

Fleming is being initiated into a cruel and violent level of reality he has not seen back on the farm, but his synchronic assumption that the battle-field should answer his protest of injustice reveals an immaturity that can be exposed in war, in a dinghy on the open sea, even in Whilomville, the small-town setting of Crane's *Whilomville Stories*. When the youth is fleeing, rationalizing, or charging ahead, he has little time for honest reflection; and the fact that his "philippic" consists of one word, "Hell" (137), shows that his initiation, at this point, is equally aborted. (In the next chapter, he commits his deepest sin: his desertion of the tattered man.) The scene, however, drama-tizes a fundamental principle in Crane's values.

For Crane, protests, pleadings, questions, and curses directed to the uni-verse are signs of immaturity and egocentricity. Fleming's abortive protest and the "red wafer" are directly comparable to an expository passage in "The Open Boat":

> When it occurs to a man that nature does not regard him as important, and that she feels she would not maim the universe by disposing of him, he at first wishes to throw bricks at the temple, and he hates deeply the fact that there are no bricks and no temples. (902)

Crane's ironic language—"maim the universe," the childish urge to "throw bricks"—makes it clear that he believes the lesson of nature's indifference is an elementary lesson needed only by the naive, the idealistic, the cynical, or the egocentric. Nature's indifference, per se, does not suggest determinism. Crane is not exposing virtue. His target is the foolish expectation that ocean waves should reward the virtue of hard work. Satirizing indulgent subjectiv-ity is Crane's signature.

Fleming's egocentricity is shown after the first charge when he finds it "surprising that Nature had gone tranquilly on with her golden process in the midst of so much devilment" (116). Other examples include Fleming's feeling that "swishing saplings tried to make known his presence to the world" (125); his "combating the universe" (172); and his recalling the time, just yesterday, "when he had *imagined* the universe to be against him" (172; emphasis added).

An important step in Fleming's progress from egocentricity toward maturity occurs when he and Wilson know an "ironical secret." The odds are that not many will survive, yet the two young friends "see no hesitation in each other's faces" (181). Fleming is learning that the inability of human beings to control events does not release them from responsibility—in this case, a soldier's obligation to perform the duty he has voluntarily undertaken.

Finally, "it came to pass" that "his [Fleming's] soul changed" (212), but Crane's frequent use of biblical language implies a humanistic rather than a Christian context. This is why Fleming can only "put the sin" of deserting the tattered man "at a distance" (212). In Crane's world, there is no benevolent deity to absolve Fleming's sins or to strengthen him against backsliding. Just moments after the youth feels a "serene self-confidence" (199), he remembers the man who called his regiment "mule drivers" and develops a self-pitying idea, "vaguely formulated, that his corpse would be for those eyes a great and salt reproach" (202).

What Fleming is struggling to overcome is a foolishly romantic and self-centered imagination that keeps him from seeing what is in front of him and from knowing himself. Teased by dreams of glory, terrified by death, and agonizing with guilt, Fleming creates distorted pictures.[9] In the first chapter, the youth's "busy mind had drawn for him large pictures extravagant in color, lurid with breathless deeds" (83). When veterans tell him tales of the ferocity of the enemy, "the youth imagine[s] the red, live bones sticking out through slits in the faded uniforms" (87).

By contrast, on the second day of fighting, "it *seemed*" to the youth that he "saw everything," including each "blade of green grass" (93; emphasis added), an exaggeration, certainly, but nonetheless a sign of his growing away from the glorious and nightmarish distortions that have characterized his whirling perceptions.

After returning to the regiment with his "red badge of courage" (133), Fleming reviews "the battle pictures he had seen." He then decides in supreme dishonesty that he has enough experience to tell tales back home that would leave "his gaping audience picturing him as the central figure in blazing scenes" (166).

In the final chapter, Fleming is beginning to purge himself of the distorted picturings of self-indulgent subjectivity: "For a time the youth was obliged to reflect in a puzzled and uncertain way. His mind *was undergoing* a subtle change. . . . Gradually *his brain emerged from the clogged clouds*, and at last he was enabled to *more closely* comprehend himself and circumstance" (210; emphasis added).

This "subtle change" is largely a matter of reflecting on his deeds in "spectator fashion," thus getting outside himself, becoming less egocentric, and developing enough honesty to "criticize" his actions "with *some* correctness" (210; emphasis added). The concluding description of Fleming's progress is not undercut by the absurdity of his earlier dreams, posturing, rationalizing, and lying. The conclusion is reportorial and valorized rather than ironic and judgmental. The conclusion also represents Fleming's, not the author's, thoughts: he "understood . . . the past"; "he began to study his deeds, his failures, and his achievements"; "he struggled to marshal all his acts" (210).

In this moment of euphoria, Fleming is certainly exaggerating. He knows the next battle will not begin his "existence of soft and eternal peace" (212), and he knows that farm work is not a lazy, pastoral life, but Fleming's moment of celebration should be read in the context of Crane's diachronic narration. In the opening chapter, Fleming's head is filled with a childish ambition for the glories of bloody conquests. In the concluding chapter, he yearns for life.

A "golden ray of sun" breaks through, but it breaks through "hosts of leaden rain clouds" (212). The soldiers, in language recalling the opening paragraph, are "a bedraggled train, despondent and muttering, marching with churning effort in a trough of liquid brown mud under a low, wretched sky" (212). Fleming, however, has learned that though suffering and death are real, so are his accomplishments and his "store of assurance" (212). He is experiencing his version of what others may learn in an open boat at sea: Both the view "from a balcony" (886), which shows human efforts to be "absurd," and the view from the boat, which reveals a brotherhood so real it "dwelt" (890) in the boat and gave off heat, are real.[10]

It is fair, I think, for Crane to have the youth enjoy his moment of celebration, his release from the torment of egocentricity and his emergence as a local hero. A "store of assurance," meaning *some* assurance, is more realistic than "[h]e knew that he would no more quail before his guides" (212), meaning *never* quail; but during this brief respite from combat, the youth is ecstatic to have "rid himself of" both the desire to be a bloodthirsty hero and the nightmarish picturings promoted by a demeaning fear of his own death. His dishonest and self-serving motives have been quelled. He is a person of worth.

In the diachronic world of Stephen Crane, both idealism and cynicism distort reality, but the distortions of such absolutes do not relieve his characters of responsibility to move, as best they can, from egocentricity toward a "personal honesty."

Notes

1. For readings fundamentally different from mine, see, for example, Conder and Kaplan. Conder (53–68) argues that any belief in the reality of values is indoctrination and therefore invalid; any negative influence is valid and therefore the truth, which is determinism. Thus, Fleming's humanistic thoughts at the end of the novel are illusions, because nature is indifferent. Kaplan holds that with the story of

the cheery soldier, "Crane makes the major turning point in his narrative gratuitous and parodies storytelling by exposing its arbitrariness" (94).

2. Shulman (202–16) argues that Crane made Fleeting a modern Everyman but included no authorial judgments. Conder also says that Fleming "is an every-man" (68). Beaver says *The Red Badge* "reads like some zany inscrutable allegory of *non-sense*" (191). Pease describes *The Red Badge* as "a series of discontinuous incidents" (157) and Fleming as a character who "perceives . . . little more than sheer impressions, unrelieved by any signification whatsoever" (158).

3. Becoming courageous in battle is an ambiguous prerequisite to the development of Fleming's character, but Dooley's insightful emphasis on morality is impressive: Fleming's

> growth to adulthood is not due to battlefield heroics and public deeds. Rather, his quiet manhood is the fruit of three separate moral realizations: his confrontation with a serious ethical choice, his acknowledgment that he had failed to respond morally, and his most difficult and humbling experience, the decision to forgive and accept himself. (*Pluralistic Philosophy* 89)

4. Solomon makes a convincing argument (220–34) that Fleming's regiment undergoes a pattern of experience similar to his own.

5. For a convenient list of essays relevant to the question of Christian symbolism, plus lists of essays on three other topics central to criticism of *The Red Badge*, see Dooley's *Stephen Crane: An Annotated Bibliography* (70–71).

6. Whatever one's interpretation of *The Red Badge* may be, Benfey's emphasis on physicality (106–19) is a valuable addition to Crane studies.

7. In "The Little Regiment," Crane's praise of "that splendor of heedlessness which belongs only to veterans" is so extreme that it could be called newspaper propaganda, but it shows that Crane admired a devotion to duty that is opposite to the whining and complaining of Fleming and Wilson (Gullason 277).

Brooke-Rose contends that Fleming's supposed courage in battle is false: "The role of color bearer that the youth so desires can be seen as the equivalent of a cheerleader—but, more importantly, it represents the position of one who does not fight" (140). A cheerleader, however, is not shot at, does not see friends being wounded and killed, and can go home at night to a hot meal and a warm bed. The color bearer's job is to stay conspicuously out front; it is difficult to duck down low or find cover when holding a flag aloft, and the enemy's flag bearer is a favorite target because the enemy's flag is a prized possession. The role is even more dangerous than that of a soldier with a rifle.

Nevertheless, I think Brooke-Rose has made a valuable insight. Choosing the role of flag bearer for Fleming may have been Crane's way of resolving his own ambiguous feelings toward war. *The Red Badge* is clearly an antiwar novel that praises courage in combat; however, "Marines Signalling under Fire at Guantanamo," "The Upturned Face," "An Episode of War," and Crane's other writings on war, along with *The Red Badge*, emphasize courage associated with duty and character rather than the type of courage represented by personally shooting a large number of enemy soldiers.

8. Osborn suggests "wafer or seal" but offers no interpretation (362, n. 3).

9. For an excellent study of picturings in Crane, see Nagel (especially 56); Brown's analysis of photographic images in *The Red Badge* is also excellent (149–59).

10. In two excised passages, Crane had Fleming deciding that the sin of deserting the tattered soldier could be made useful by "hindering the workings of his egotism"; that the "machinery of the universe" was a "deity laying about him with the bludgeon of correction"; and that "[i]n the space-wide whirl of events no grain like him would be lost" (most commonly available in Stallman 369).

Fleming does seem to be taught, in part, by "the bludgeon of correction." However, I believe Crane was right to omit these two passages, because they come too close to being messages from the author, rather than the youth's ecstatic celebration, and because they are inaccurate to the novel and to Crane's own credo. To say that the "machinery of the universe" is a "deity" with the purpose of correcting Henry Fleming is to repudiate Crane's fundamental belief in the indifference of nature. Bullets in warfare, like waves in "The Open Boat," do not reward good and punish evil. One wave rescues the correspondent; an undertow, or something, kills the oiler. Circumstance is mindless, not a "deity."

Developing the courage to go forward in the face of injustice is essential to maturation in the world of Stephen Crane. Also, the statement that "no grain like him would be lost" ignores Jim Conklin, Maggie, Tommie, and others who are "lost" through no fault of their own.

Works Cited

Beaver, Harold. "Stephen Crane: The Hero as Victim." Spec. issue of *The Yearbook of English Studies* 12 (1982): 186–93. Ed. G. K. Hunter and C. J. Rawson. Great Britain: Modern Humanities Research Association, 1982.

Benfey, Christopher. *The Double Life* of *Stephen Crane: A Biography*. New York: Knopf, 1992.

Brooke-Rose, Christine. "Ill Logics of Irony." Mitchell 129–46.

Brown, Bill. *The Material Unconscious: American Amusement, Stephen Crane, & the Economies of Play*. Cambridge, MA: Harvard UP, 1996.

Conder, John J. *Naturalism in American Fiction: The Classic Phase*. Lexington: The UP of Kentucky, 1984.

Crane, Stephen. *Maggie*. Levenson 7–78.

———. "The Open Boat." Levenson 885–909.

———. *The Red Badge of Courage*. Levenson 81–212.

Dooley, Patrick K. *The Pluralistic Philosophy of Stephen Crane*. Chicago: U of Illinois P, 1999.

———. *Stephen Crane: An Annotated Bibliography of Secondary Scholarship*. New York: G. K. Hall, 1992.

Gullason, Thomas A., ed. *The Complete Short Stories and Sketches of Stephen Crane*. Garden City, NY: Doubleday, 1963.

Kaplan, Amy. "The Spectacle of War in Crane's Revision of History." Mitchell 77–108.

Levenson, J. C., ed. *Stephen Crane: Prose and Poetry*. New York: Library Classics of the United States, 1984. Selected from *The University of Virginia Edition of the Works of Stephen Crane*. Charlottesville: UP of Virginia, 1969–1975.

Mitchell, Lee Clark, ed. *New Essays on* The Red Badge of Courage. New York: Cambridge UP, 1986.

Nagel, James. *Stephen Crane and Literary Impressionism*. University Park: Pennsylvania State UP, 1980.

Osborn, Scott C. "Stephen Crane's Imagery: 'Pasted Like a Wafer.'" *American Literature* 23 (1951): 362.

Pease, Donald. "Fear, Rage, and the Mistrials of Representation in *The Red Badge of Courage*." *American Realism: New Essays*. Ed. Eric J. Sundquist. Baltimore: Johns Hopkins UP, 1982. 155–75.

Shulman, Robert. "*The Red Badge of Courage* and Social Violence: Crane's Myth of His America." *Critical Essays on Stephen Crane's The Red Badge of Courage*. Ed. Donald Pizer. Boston: G. K. Hall, 1990. 202–16. Reprinted from *Canadian Review of American Studies* 12 (Spring 1981): 1–19.

Solomon, Eric. "The Structure of *The Red Badge of Courage*." *Modern Fiction Studies* 5 (1959): 220–34.

Stallman, Robert Wooster, ed. *Stephen Crane: An Omnibus*. New York: Knopf, 1952.

Wertheim, Stanley, and Paul Sorrentino, eds. *The Correspondence of Stephen Crane*. Vol. 1. New York: Columbia UP, 1988.

BENJAMIN F. FISHER

The Red Badge of Courage
under British Spotlights Again

These pages provide information that augments my previous publications concerning discoveries about contemporaneous British opinions of *The Red Badge of Courage*. I am confident that what appears in this and my earlier article [WLA Special Issue 1999] on the subject offers a mere fraction of such materials, given, for example, the large numbers of daily newspapers published in London alone during the 1890s. Files of many British periodicals and newspapers from the Crane era are no longer extant, principally because of bomb damage to repositories of such materials during wartime. The commentary garnered below, however, amplifies our knowledge relating to Crane's perennially compelling novel, and thus, I trust, it should not go unrecorded. If one wonders why, after a century, such a look backward might be of value to those interested in Crane, I cite a letter of Ford Maddox Ford to Paul Palmer, 11 December 1935, in which he states that Crane, along with Henry James, W.H. Hudson, and Joseph Conrad all "exercised an enormous influence on English—and later, American writing. . . ." Ford's thoughts concerning Crane's importance were essentially repeated in a later letter, to the editor of the *Saturday Review of Literature*.[1] Despite many unreliabilities in what Ford put into print on any subject, he thoroughly divined the Anglo-American literary climate from the 1890s to the 1930s. His ideas are representative of views of Crane in British eyes during

From *War, Literature, and the Arts* 12, no. 2 (Fall–Winter 2000): 203–12. Copyright © 2000 by Benjamin F. Fisher.

that era and, for that matter, views that have maintained currency to the present time.

Here's a keynote opener: "It takes [him] by the throat and keeps him motionless, horrorstruck, with great distended eyes, till the last lurid page is reached." This passage may initially suggest that the topic is a piece of fiction by Mrs. Radcliffe or Poe, or, perhaps, one of the many parodies of Gothic fiction. In fact, it comes from an 1896 review, by "Barbara," of *The Red Badge of Courage* in *Woman*, a popular weekly from the 1890s. To give proper context for the passage, a more extended version ought to clarify. Crane's book is called

> [O]ne of the most extraordinary novels of modern times. Only it is not a novel at all! It is merely an account rendered, with ruthless veracity, of a young soldier's experiences in battle. It takes the reader by the throat and keeps him motionless, horrorstruck, with great distended eyes, till the last lurid page is reached. The war pictures in Zola's *La Débacle* are milk and water beside it, and Tolstoi's *War and Peace* surpasses it only in breadth of view, a quality which Mr. Crane evidently did not aim at. The writing is extremely vivid. Take this: "The sun was a red wafer pasted on the sky." I believe Mr. Crane is an American; America has reason to feel proud of him.

"Barbara" would again acclaim *The Red Badge* not only a "startling success," but a production "that would add glory to the literature of any country." Still later "Barbara" used Crane's book as a norm against which Frank Wilkeson's *The Soldier in Battle, or, Life in the Ranks of the Army of the Potomac* (Bellairs) "reads just a little tamely."[2]

This early review of *The Red Badge* contains opinions which would reverberate throughout responses from the British on through the reissue as part of the collection published by Heinemann in July 1898 entitled *Pictures of War*—with an "appreciation" by George Wyndham, who had earlier commended the book in the columns of the *New Review*—and those separate appearances in 1900, one published by Heinemann in England, and in America by Appleton, this latter introduced by Ripley Hitchcock, who had read Crane's manuscript as Appleton's literary adviser.[3] Without great changes, many opinions found in these contemporaneous readings of *The Red Badge* still stand as eminently credible viewpoints; therefore, placing them on record is worthwhile. Critical explications of the sun as red wafer passage alone, for example, have mounted to great proportions.

Overall, British advocates of *The Red Badge* highlighted its excellence as a war novel that matched or outshined those of Tolstoi and Zola, and that ranked with Kipling's *The Light That Failed*. Indeed, a *Leeds Mercury* writer thought that Crane had "leaped suddenly to fame not long ago as the Rudyard Kipling of military romance in America." Psychological excellences also distinguished this novel from much other war fiction. Repeatedly, too, *The Red Badge* was called a "study," a term which by the 1890s had become synonymous with psychological fiction. Close to this mode of thinking, Spencer Leigh Hughes, writing in the *Gentlewoman*, commended *The Red Badge* thus: "The reverse side of the picture of [military] glory has been given with great point and incision, vividly and lucidly described." Apparently, one "needs the fascination and excitement of actual bloodshed to overcome the instinct of unreasoning panic which attacks the recruit when the bullets first rain about him and the cannon mow down his fellows in scores." The story has "great descriptive power, and more than average merit."[4]

Hughes also analyzed *The Red Badge* so as to align it with the increasing interest in the non-rational emotions "which impel humans to hostility, violence, and, at times, indifference toward the wounded and dying." Just so, the emphasis on character instead of numerous characters meshed with a clamor *for* and accomplishments *in* brevity within novels. As is evident in the opinion of Barbara quoted above, many readers found in *The Red Badge* no genuine novel at all; instead, as if citing Crane's own subtitle, they read it as an "episode," another familiar literary term in the era, as was "sketch" for a brief work of fiction. *The Red Badge*, as well as most of Crane's other work, was representative of 1890s miniaturizations in the arts. In such evaluations of the novel as these, we may detect backgrounds of the British interest in soldiery and, a related subject, the empire. Such concerns were likewise reflected, for example, in the writings of Kipling or the poems of A.E. Housman and Henry Newbolt, not to mention the continual outpourings of jingoistic verse and other writings, which highlighted imperialism and the military, in the British press. The brevity in *The Red Badge* would also have appealed to those spearheaders of the end-of-the-century efforts to do away with the ponderous triple-decker novels that had for years domineered the fiction marketplace.

Next we return to remarks earlier quoted about "vivid" writing, that is, pictorialism, in *The Red Badge*, as well as Crane's being an American and an author of whom his nation could be deservedly proud. Such distinctions also recurred among British commentators. The Anglo-American cultural world had witnessed minglings of written word and visual art from the emergence of the Pre-Raphaelites and others, such as Laurence Housman, Whistler, or the *Yellow Book* coterie, who on through the 1890s contributed materially to the collapsing of literary genres and combinations of literature with other arts. An example of what were then deplored as the extremes to which such new art could be taken, Stanley V. Makower's experimental novel, *The Mirror*

of Music (1895) in places substituted musical scores for words to express the
heroine's emotional vicissitudes which eventually ran to madness. Crane's
visual effects and his fragmentary language, in *The Red Badge* and elsewhere,
resemble those in contemporaneous novels like Thomas Hardy's *The Well-
Beloved* (1897) or Ernest Henham's weird tale of vampirism, *Tenebrae* (1898),
which many reviewers thought was incoherent, and it adumbrates such
impressionistic techniques as those employed by Ford Maddox Ford, Virginia
Woolf, Henry Miller or Thomas Pynchon during the twentieth century.

Moreover, Crane's being an American brought his works under another
type of scrutiny from British critics who found American literature worth
attention (even when they were not wholly won by its aims or methods) and,
under that umbrella, what they deemed the decidedly American language features within a particular specimen. Crane's, and other Americans', language
was often spotlighted by British reviewers, who were quick to point out diction and syntax imbued with what they thought were regionalisms and collo-
quialisms. Such attentiveness to diction and regionalisms was not confined to
notices of American writings. British writers like J.M. Barrie and others, who
were seen as members of the "Kailyard School" (Scots regionalist), or Edith
Nesbit, whose short-story collection, *In Homespun* (1896), one of John Lane's
notorious Keynotes Series volumes, was cited for its south Kentish dialect,
also came in for strictures about their language. Several years later, evaluating another of Crane's war novels, *Active Service*, Desmond B. O'Brien found
everything but its style enjoyable; most of Crane's "Americanisms will seem
to you barbarous," he wrote, but such barbarism is a "small matter compared
with the real, and sometimes dazzling, brilliancy of the novel," a compliment
that might also be paid to *The Red Badge*.[5]

An interesting laudatory and extended notice from early 1896, which
foregrounds some of the features already acknowledged, and which should
not be ignored, appeared in the *Newcastle Daily Chronicle*.[6] First, the reviewer
credited Crane with contributing "a new and important chapter in the literature of war," which supplemented those novels, by Tolstoi and Zola, already
mentioned in other notices. Tellingly, the Newcastle journalist added: "We
are apt to think less of the glorious charge than of the sickening things under
the hoofs." *The Red Badge* also makes us realize "how the soldier feels. The
theory of the loss of consciousness in the rage of battle—of the martial inspiration that comes with the thunder of the captains and the shouting—no
longer accounts for everything in the days of long-distance fighting when
there is so much slow work amidst the smoke." *The Red Badge* "is a penetrating study of the psychology of the modern soldier under fire. The book
does a ruthless work of disillusionment, but it is convincing at bottom. . . ."
Next, Crane's expression is considered: his "style is unconventional. It tries to

appear unliterary. It is plain and hard, summary and brutal. It is as if he had written, so to speak, not with a pen but with the end of a charred stick." This bit of expression very much resembled Crane's own.

Henry is, of course, the "subject of a psychological study," the "thing that looks on from within the soldier and notes everything that is passing within him and around, while the thing that the soldier knows in ordinary life as himself, works like an automaton." We in the era of the millennium may need to be reminded that stream-of-consciousness or interior monologue were, a century ago, not yet developed and refined to the degree that twentieth-century writers like James Joyce or William Faulkner were to take them, and so this contemporaneous description of Crane's methods is important. Similar effects were being singled out in some critiques of fiction by George Meredith or Henry James, among older writers, or, from the 1890s proper, by fiction from the pens of Ella D'Arcy, "George Egerton" (Mrs. Golding Bright), Gertrude Hall, or May Sinclair, to name but a few.

The Newcastle critic remarked two more imposing specifics in *The Red Badge*:

> This book is full of powerful pictures. It is indubitably one of the things that influence literature; and it is safe to say that any man of brains writing about battles will write somewhat differently after reading "The Red Badge of Courage." We do not say that it contains the truth. But the unconvincing touches are very few; and it contains a very great deal of the truth.

Once again attention is directed toward Crane's accomplishments in pictorialism and in realism and, implicitly, to what has indeed proved to be the influence of his novel. Anent this type of evaluation, we might turn to the *Yorkshire Post*, which found *The Red Badge* "a striking story of the American Civil War. It offers but a glimpse or two; and is rather a study in cowardice and courage than in anything else. But its realism lays hold of the reader, and makes him wish the author had given us more story and less analysis."[7] This commentary touches on staccato effects in *The Red Badge*, as well as foregrounding its realism. Like thinking informs T.P. O'Connor's "A Book of the Week" critique in the *Weekly Sun*, where, along with an extensive plot summary, *The Red Badge* was complimented for rousing deserved enthusiasm, adding that the "keynote" is struck on page one to bring down war to "its true, prosaic, everyday level." Here is a "fine piece of literary work which strips the battlefield of all its false glory, and shows it in all its foulness and bestiality...."[8] O'Connor's concluding remark might well enter Crane's novel into the camp of Naturalism set up by George Moore or Arthur Morrison, whose works created a ruckus among British readers and critics during the last years of the nineteenth century. Concurrence sounded from the *Leeds Mercury* reviewer of *The Third Violet*, who thought that Crane's reputation had "been honestly won by a distinction of style and a certain dramatic realism of a remarkable kind." Similar outlook was expressed by "Lector," in the *New Age*, several weeks later: Noting that Crane's work (his "good verse" was also noticed) defies tradition, he stated that the American had "revealed the utter hideousness of warfare as no writer has yet done."[9]

Other evaluations were more chary in their commendation. The *Bradford Observer* viewed *The Red Badge* as an "episode of the American Civil War . . . which gives evidence of much careful work . . . but it is questionable whether an analysis of the feelings of a soldier in time of war will do more than interest a limited number of readers." This newspaper did not review many books, and so its objectivity in measuring excellence and weakness indicates that British response to *The Red Badge* was not so consistently wholehearted as some more recent scholars suggest. Nonetheless, one wonders what the Bradford writer might think, were he writing a century later about war fiction, and had he read Hemingway, Heller, and many more fiction writers whose subject is indeed the "soldier in time of war." In *Pictures of War*, according to the *Liverpool Daily Post*, and "[f]ar transcending the other six [sketches] in length," *The Red Badge* is "marked by a microscopic attention to detail—analytical, indeed, almost to tediousness." Nevertheless, "remarkable ability" is evident. Assessing the same version of *The Red Badge*, Desmond B. O'Brien stated: "The fault you would find . . . [is] that it makes its hero all eyes and ears and nerves, and that only a biograph, or whatever the camera for taking animated photographs is called, could record so many and transient and vivid pictures in so short a time. But the pictures themselves are wonderful. If they have a fault it is that of a constant and conscious strain at effect, which . . . sometimes defeats itself." Furthermore, as I have noted elsewhere, the *Lady's Pictorial*, no matter what accolades it accorded Crane's books, never missed an opportunity to hit at his use of profanities. Conversely, the *Weekly Sun* reviewer thought that *Pictures of War* displayed how Crane managed "to see and hear, and record much that would escape the eyes and ears of the average soldier."[10]

Whether the British found *The Red Badge* wholly artistic or guilty of blemishes, reviewers seldom failed to compare Crane's other works with that book. The *Leeds Mercury* critic of *The Third Violet* found validity in the old saying about a cobbler sticking to his last, and deplored the falloff in "strength and imaginative form" from *The Red Badge* in the later novel. Spencer Leigh Hughes likewise deprecated *The Third Violet*: "coming from the author of 'The Red Badge of Courage,' this story is a disappointment," despite its being "an original work and well put together." Later, Hughes would measure approvingly with the same yardstick: "To say that the author of 'The Red Badge of Courage' has given us another of his excellent productions is the best recommendation of 'The Open Boat'." Kindred sentiments echo in an obituary notice in the *Daily News*, where *The Red Badge* was applauded as an intensely "realistic study of the psychology of war. . . . The book is full not only of vivid and harrowing descriptions, but of the keenest analyses of conduct and motive and emotion. Similar powers of psychological portrayal permeate "[The] Open Boat."[11]

What unfolds above shows some overlooked parts of what Joseph Conrad dubbed the "noisy recognition" in Great Britain of *The Red Badge*, the book which, as the *Dundee Advertiser* forecast, "the late Stephen Crane will be remembered by . . . it remains a remarkable piece of literature, and the best example of that style of writing in which its lamented writer excelled." Hard upon Crane's death, the *Morning Post* reviewer of *Bowery Tales* praised *Maggie*, calling it "as admirable in its own field as 'The Red Badge of Courage' in another." Certain parts of *Wounds in the Rain* also compared favorably with *The Red Badge*, a reviewer for the *St. James's Gazette* believed, although the later stories did not attain the "same irresistible sequence of things, nor the pauseless, violent sweep of thought and deed which made 'The Red Badge' wonderful."

The general British feeling toward *The Red Badge* at the time is perhaps well summed up in the *Daily Chronicle* shortly after Crane's death: "There is to be a sixpenny edition of the late Mr. Stephen Crane's best-known and best book, 'The Red Badge of Courage.' Mr. Heinemann first issued this book in his Pioneer Series in the autumn of 1895. The result was the 'discovery' of Mr. Crane in the larger sense, for it means beyond all doubt that the 'Red Badge' only 'boomed' in America after it had made a hit here."[12] Thence we might turn, fittingly, to a critique of the Heinemann edition of 1900. There, Crane's pictorial achievements and his excellent psychological portrayals of men in battle are centralized as interlocking techniques. We are made aware, offered this commentator, of "all that passes through the mind of the lad, the ambition, the cowardice, the sinking of heart, the shame, the recovery. We begin to understand how panics arise, how battles are won and lost, and how in the stress of fight men become possessed with fierce abnormal strength, and with the passions of heroes and brutes." These observations epitomize much that was expressed elsewhere. On occasion, long after they were set forth, such century-old opinions, time and again, reveal anticipations of much that have emerged as continuing valid approaches to the work of Stephen Crane. Forty years ago Walter E. Houghton wrote that "to look into the Victorian mind is to see some primary sources of the modern mind."[13] What I have outlined above upholds that precept, and, I trust, contributes bibliographically and critically to Crane studies.

NOTES

1. See my "*The Red Badge of Courage* under British Spotlights," *War, Literature & the Arts* [*Stephen Crane in War and Peace* special issue (1999)]: 72–81; and my "Transatlantic Stephen Crane," *English Literature in Transition*, 42.3 (1999): 349. Ford's opinions appear in *Letters of Ford Madox Ford*, ed. Richard M. Ludwig. Princeton, N.J.: Princeton UP, 1965: 248, 302. Elsewhere, Ford designated Crane as the "immensely successful author" of *The Red Badge*, noting, too that that book was a "best seller of fantastic proportions." See Ford's *Return to Yesterday*. New York: Horace Liveright, 1932: respectively 66, 56; and, allowing for its imperfections in other respects, R.W. Stallman's confirmation of the great attention accorded *The Red Badge* in Great Britain, in *Stephen Crane: A Biography*. rev. ed. New York: George Braziller, 1973: 181–187. I acknowledge the kindness of Professor Donald Vanouse in offering me a forum during a session of the Stephen Crane Society in May of 1999, for the ideas expressed here. I also acknowledge gratitude to Professor James H. Meredith for encouraging my continuing explorations of the British on *The Red Badge*; and to my wife, Julie A. Fisher, for technological assistance.

2. Barbara, "Book Chat," *Woman*, 1 January 1896: 6; 26 February 1896: 6; 8 April 1896: 7.

3. Wyndham, "A Remarkable Book," *New Review*, 14 (January 1896): 30–40. The question of superiority between Appleton's 1895 version of *The Red Badge* and the version found in manuscript has continued to provoke controversy among Crane scholars.

4. "Literary Arrivals," *Leeds Mercury*, 2 August 1897: 3; Sub Rosa, "Under Cover," *Gentlewoman*, 1 February 1896: 123. Davenport Adams, in "Books and Things Bookish," *Whitehall Review*, 26 September 1896: 13–14, also called *Maggie* a "study."

5. "Letters on Books," *Truth*, 21 December 1899: 1567.

6. "In All Moods. Some Recent Novels," *Newcastle Daily Chronicle*, 28 January 1896: 4.

7. "Books to Read and Books to Use," *Yorkshire Post*, 4 March 1896: 6.

8. "A Book of the Week," *Weekly Sun*, 8 March 1896: 1–2.

9. "Literary Life," *New Age*, 19 March 1896: 390; cf. the *Leeds Mercury* citation in n4 above.

10. "Some Recent Books," *Liverpool Daily Post*, 2 November 1898: 7; "Fiction," *Bradford Observer*, 21 January 1896: 6. Despite this stinting portrayal, the *Bradford Observer* characterized Crane as "the author of *The Red Badge of Courage*" in reviewing *The Little Regiment*, "Literature," 2 April 1897: 6, and also quashed a rumor that Crane had died in a shipwreck. See also Desmond B. O'Brien, "Letters on Books," *Truth*, 1 September 1898: 557. O'Brien found the style in the *Pictures* overdone: "Such phrases as 'red cheers,' 'a crimson roar' (confirmatory, by the way, of the idea of that blind man cited by Locke who thought red was like the sound of a trumpet) seem forced; while there is neither dignity nor expressiveness in such images as this: 'They were ever upraising the ghost of shame on the stick of their curiosity.' I begin to despair of ever seeing the last of the misusage of 'ilk'—which means simply 'the same'—in such sentences as this: 'In battle every one would surely run, save forlorn

hopes and their ilk.' This, however, is mere pedantry, and so fine a book as Mr. Stephen Crane's 'Pictures of War' is not to be judged pedantically." See also my "*The Red Badge of Courage* under British Spotlights," cited in n1: 76; and "Pictures of War," *Weekly Sun*, 4 September 1898: 2.

11. "Sub Rosa," "Under Cover," *Gentlewoman*, 25 April 1897: 383; 30 July 1898: 140. See also the review of *The Third Violet* in the *Leeds Mercury*, cited in n4 above; "Death of Mr. Stephen Crane," *Daily News*, 6 June 1900: 7.

12. Conrad's words are quoted by Frederic Whyte, *William Heinemann: A Memoir*. London: Jonathan Cape, 1928: 170, wherein *The Red Badge* is also designated "one of Heinemann's outstanding successes in 1895. . . ." The Scottish columnist's acclaim appears in a review of Heinemann's 1900 sixpenny edition—"General Literature," *Dundee Advertiser*, 16 August 1900: 2. See also "The Last of Stephen Crane," *St. James's Gazette*, 27 September 1900: 6; "Fiction and Fact," *Morning Post*, 28 June 1900: 2; "Writers and Readers," *Daily Chronicle*, 6 July 1900: 3. The *Daily Chronicle* review might have been more tempered toward Americans on *The Red Badge*, had its author read, for example, "Books and Authors," in the *Boston Courier*, 20 October 1895: 2, the ideas in which dovetail with those in many British commentaries. Stallman cites, but does not annotate, this interesting review—*Stephen Crane: A Critical Bibliography*. Ames, Iowa: Iowa State UP, 1972: 84, note at the beginning of entries for *The Red Badge*.

13. Outlaw, "Holiday Literature," *New Age*, 16 August 1900: 517; Walter E. Houghton, *The Victorian Frame of Mind 1830–1870*. New Haven, London: Yale UP, 1957, p. xiv.

ANDREW LAWSON

The Red Badge of Class:
Stephen Crane and the Industrial Army

In the midst of what became known as the Great Depression of 1873 to 1896, the economist David Ames Wells noted that 'a series of widespread and complex disturbances' were affecting the American economy.[1] Wells laid the blame for falling profits, increasing labour unrest, and intensified competition between nation states on what was already well-known as 'overproduction.' A given amount of labour, 'operating through machinery,' now produced 'at least a third more product' in a given time.[2] The burden of 'interest, insurance, and care' entailed in high-volume, mechanized production meant that the owner naturally desired 'to convert outlay into income by utilizing it to the greatest extent possible,' thus flooding the market with goods and driving prices down.[3] But the size and economic power of a modern industrial enterprise meant that it could stay in the market even while receiving prices below costs, so driving out smaller producers. This strategy works well in good times, when credit is cheap, but if supply runs too far in excess of demand, and credit becomes restricted, enterprises find themselves over-extended and are forced into liquidation. The result is a cycle of 'panic and speculation, of trade activity and stagnation.'[4] When linear progress becomes involved in recurrent cycles of boom and bust, it is difficult for the citizens of an advanced capitalist democracy to know where exactly they are: on an upturn or a downturn, a beginning or an ending. Under the new

From *Literature and History* 14, no. 2 (October 2005): 53–68. Copyright © 2005 by Manchester University Press.

conditions of modern industrial production, the equilibrium of supply and demand is disturbed and the social order plunged into a condition of permanent crisis, a 'protracted economic derangement.'[5]

Henry Fleming, the ambiguous hero of Stephen Crane's novel, *The Red Badge of Courage* (1895), finds himself in a similar state of disequilibrium. As Amy Kaplan notes, the novel is marked by a lack of any 'cohesive narrative pattern,' by the absence of 'a traditional plot with logical sequence and causality.'[6] The instabilities of the novel concern both Henry and the military action he is involved in. Henry alternates between wildly fluctuating moods of heroism and cowardice, compulsively plunging into the battle, and, just as compulsively, fleeing it. The battle itself obeys no logic or pattern, being composed of 'a series of charges and countercharges, advances and retreats,' with no apparent goal or purpose.[7] 'Nobody seems to know where we go or why we go,' Henry complains at one point, '[w]e just get fired around from pillar to post [...] and nobody knows what it's done for.'[8] The disordered war the novel depicts is compared directly to the economic cycle when Henry observes a 'much harassed' general surveying the progress of the battle with 'the appearance of a businessman whose market is swinging up and down' (p. 39).

These analogies between war and industrial crisis are developed further in *The Red Badge of Courage* and the journalism Crane produced during his writing of the novel, in the period between the spring of 1893 and the spring of the following year.[9] I shall argue that the novel marks an intervention into a historical conflict, not so much between North and South, but between what Martin J. Sklar refers to as the 'emerging corporate-capitalist order' and its opponents: industrial workers and small producers.[10] Crane is drawn towards an identification, not with screeching generals, but with the tattered men of the industrial army. What makes this identification a problematic and ambivalent one are the pressures exerted by 'progressive' or corporate publishing, with its aim of reaching a mass market, as well as Crane's own desire for success.

I

Overproduction and disequilibrium are abstract enough as processes, but they had concrete results. On 20 February 1893, the Philadelphia and Reading Railroad went bankrupt with debts of over $125 million, an ominous sign of what was to come. On the 4th of May the National Cordage Company failed. The next day, 'Black Friday,' crowds filled the galleries of the New York Stock Exchange, 'anticipating a panic and a flood of selling orders.' Within minutes, 'leading stocks plunged to record lows, amid pandemonium on the floor and in the streets outside.'[11] As banks called in loans from overextended companies there were more business failures: an average of two dozen a day. A wave of railroad bankruptcies meant that thirty two steel corporations went out of business in the first six months of the year. Five hundred banks and sixteen thousand businesses closed during the year as a whole. The number of unemployed was estimated at between two and three million, at least one-fifth of the industrial work-force.[12] In New York, a police poll counted over 67,000 residents unemployed, together with 20,000 homeless and vagrant.[13] A spokesman for the organized charities of New York reported that '[s]ome communities when the hard times came this winter, and the army of the unemployed swept through the streets, were panic-stricken, the inhabitants fortified themselves behind soup-houses, threw loaves of bread out upon the besiegers; naturally the siege continued.'[14]

In the spring of 1894 the crisis intensified. 'The tramps walk the land like the squalid spectres of the laborers who once tilled it,' William Dean Howells observed in the *North American Review*; '[t]he miners have swarmed up out of their pits, to starve in the open air.'[15] Groups of unemployed workers in the West began organizing themselves along military lines and took to the road as 'industrial armies.' The most publicized of these industrial armies was the group of 122 'unemployed barbers, cooks, miners, and laborers' led by Jacob S. Coxey, who began a march from Massillon, Ohio to Washington on Easter Sunday, 25 March, demanding a federal works programme for the relief of the unemployed, financed by an issue of non-interest bearing bonds.[16] The colours of the American flag were borne by a young black man from West Virginia, Jasper Johnson. Coxey's sixteen-year old son, Jesse, rode in a troop of mounted men, wearing 'a coat of Union blue and pants of Confederate gray,' symbolizing the sectional unity of the nation's unemployed.[17] Apparently alert to the intended symbolism, the New York police superintendent, Thomas Byrnes, warned the readers of the *North American Review* that Coxey's movement was the 'most dangerous this country has seen since the Civil War.'[18]

Panic, armies, besieged cities: it doesn't take a great leap of the imagination to see why Crane should begin a novel ostensibly 'about' the Civil War at this particular moment of crisis. But what is striking is the way in which the events of 1893–94 resonate with the key tropes of contemporary political discourse, or what might be called the Populist imaginary. For some time it had seemed to many Americans, particularly small farmers, that they were engaged in a war with the emerging corporate order. The movement which became known as Populism mobilized the foot soldiers of the 'people' against the 'plutocracy,' the 'producers' against the parasitic 'money-power.' A tide of agrarian radicalism swept the South, as well as the Western states of Nebraska, Missouri, and the Dakota Territory, as farmers felt the crippling effects of low prices for their crops and high costs for credit. A mass folk movement, replete with pamphlets and parades, ballads and debates, had come into existence, a movement driven by a chiliastic sense of injustice, of an impending showdown between 'Corporate Greed and the great Plain People.'[19] At a Denver rally in July, 1894, the Populist governor of Colorado, Davis H. Waite, declared that 'the war' against the 'money power' had begun, and that it was 'better, infinitely better, that blood should flow to the horses bridles than our national liberties should be destroyed.'[20]

Populism's claims to be a radical movement were contested in the early 1890s. Samuel Gompers, President of the American Federation of Labor, described the People's Party as representing only '*employing* farmers,' with no regard for 'the interests of the *employed* farmers of the country districts or the mechanics and laborers of the industrial centres.'[21] A main current in the history of Populism has backed Gompers's judgement, arguing that, for all its token gestures towards the eight hour day movement, Populism was dedicated to the 'strengthening of competitive capitalism,' and to the 'salvation of small enterprise,' rather than the salvation of the wage earner.[22] But some Populists were wage earners. From Kansas and Nebraska in particular, militant voices could be heard protesting against a wage system 'which subjects the laborer in the field, in the shop or mine, to the merciless and soulless moneyed corporation as to what he is to receive for the products of his labor.'[23] In the early months of 1894, economic distress and the emergence of the industrial armies brought agrarian and urban protest together, forcing the issue of exploitation into the light of day. A developing 'industrial or class awareness' in the West was made manifest when, in February, Governor Waite ordered the state militia to protect striking miners at Cripple Creek against an army of strike-breakers.[24] In New York, the Central Labor Union hailed Coxey's Army as the 'forerunner of a great uprising of the toilers of America.'[25] For a moment, a 'new class war' seemed to have broken out, reviving 'millenarian visions' of 'the freeing of wage slaves.'[26]

It is this repressed salience of class that erupts in the spectral appearance of the industrial armies. The official historian of Coxey's Army, Henry Vincent, begins by pleading that the marchers 'are not armies of tramps and ragamuffins,' but 'Americans, decent Americans, seeking to attain a more than justifiable end by justifiable means.'[27] But Vincent goes on to use a most un-American term, describing Coxey's Army as 'this gigantic movement of the proletariat in the year of our Lord, 1894.'[28] The signifier 'proletarian,' as opposed to 'the people,' thus refers to that class of workers whose position in the division of labour is characterized by exploitation and insecurity. Forced to yield up his or her labour as a commodity on the upturn of the cycle, the proletarian is thrown back into the ranks of the 'reserve army' of the unemployed when the downturn hits.[29] It is these aspects of a newly visible proletarian identity which inform Crane's perspective on the contemporary crisis, and his novel of the Civil/industrial war.

II

As he was writing *The Red Badge of Courage*, recreating a Civil War which was being recreated around him, Crane was also producing newspaper stories on depression-hit New York. 'An Experiment in Misery,' which appeared over the page from a story about Coxey's advance on Washington in the New York *Press* on 22 April 1894, is the record of Crane's insertion into the Populist imaginary and the proletarian experience.[30]

The piece begins with a dialogue between two men who are 'regarding,' that is to say, looking at, 'a tramp.' One of them wonders 'how he [the tramp] feels,' but judging that it is 'idle to speculate from a distance,' he decides to 'try it' for himself by adopting '[r]ags and tatters.' 'Perhaps I could discover his point of view or something near it,' he says.[31] The disguised 'youth' loiters in City Hall Park, eats soup in a Chatham Street saloon, and goes in search of a cheap boarding house for the night. The boarding house is initially resistant to the youth's understanding, 'a black, opaque interior' filled with 'vast masses of tumbled shadows' which resolve into the shapes of sleeping men (p. 287). But '[w]ithin reach of the youth's hand' lies a man 'with yellow breast and shoulders bare to the cold drafts.' The passage continues:

> Beneath the inky brows could be seen the eyes of the man exposed by the partly opened lids. To the youth it seemed that he and this corpse-like being were exchanging a prolonged stare and that the other threatened with his eyes. He drew back, watching his neighbor from the shadows of his blanket edge. (p. 288)

Why should the other threaten with his eyes? Among the group of things called 'uncanny' Freud includes 'doubts whether an apparently animate being is really alive, or conversely, whether a lifeless object might not be in fact animate.'[32] The uncanny, Freud goes on, involves 'something which is familiar and old-established in the mind and which has become alienated from it only through the process of repression;' 'something which ought to have remained hidden but has come to light;' 'something repressed which recurs.'[33] The psychic mechanism involved in the uncanny is projection, 'the urge to project material outward as something foreign to the self.'[34] It is because the repressed returns 'from the outside' that it appears both familiar and strange, fascinating and appalling. But what is the traumatic 'something' which is being repressed and, simultaneously, coming to light in Crane's text?

The uncanny exchange of stares between the sightless tramp and the seeing youth produces an effect of recognition where there has been only distance and opacity. The 'long wails' of another sleeping man, 'high piercing beginnings that dwindled to final melancholy moans,' at last enable the youth to grasp 'the meaning of the room and its occupants' (pp. 288, 288–89):

> It was to him the protest of the wretch who feels the touch of the imperturbable granite wheels and who then cries with an impersonal eloquence, with a strength not from him, giving voice to the wail of a whole section, a class, a people. (p. 289)

The middle term here—class—is the least expected, the most jarring. There is, after all, a long tradition of regarding class consciousness as alien to American society because of that society's unique promise of upward mobility: a tradition captured by Lincoln's declaration that 'the man who labored for another last year this year labors for himself, and next year he will hire others to labor for him.'[35] But Crane has to use 'class' because what he is describing is a moment of historical crisis in which the industrial army becomes visible as a class acting 'for itself,' a moment when tramps stalk the land and miners swarm from the ground, a moment in which the battle lines of the industrial war appear sharply drawn.[36] What is remarkable about the youth's experiment in misery, which could have turned out to be merely a voyeuristic exercise in 'cross-identity inhabitation,' is that the youth begins to identify not with 'the people,' but specifically with the industrial proletariat.[37] Cross-class dressing becomes cross-class identification, as the youth begins to recognize in the return 'from the outside' of the proletarian the repressed roots of his own identity.

The distance the youth had felt between himself and the boarding house men now becomes a distance between himself and the middle classes. As he sits in the park the next day, the youth watches well-dressed people pass without seeing them:

> They expressed to the young man his infinite distance from all that he valued. Social position, comfort, the pleasures of living, were unconquerable kingdoms. He felt a sudden awe. (p. 293)

It is a historical commonplace that, in the Gilded Age, 'the conflict between capital and labor was getting bloodier at the seams of a hardened class structure.'[38] But, as Eric Schocket notes, during the depression of the

1890s, the 'lines between "tramps" and workers, between skilled American craftspeople and recent immigrants, blurred under the pressure of penury's seemingly indiscriminate mobility. The once secure native working class and the emergent middle class seemed suddenly at risk from the rising tide of massive unemployment.'[39] Many Americans were asking themselves the question posed by a North Wichita man in a letter to the Kansas Governor, Lorenzo D. Lewelling, whose proclamation of 4 December 1893 became known as the 'Tramp Circular:' '[w]ho does *not* bear constantly with him the dark spector [sic], that by another year perhaps he and his may be *vagrants* [?]'[40] For Schocket, class transvestism 'deconstructs class,' which is 'constructed now through the production and replication of cultural signs rather than through the shared experience of economic exploitation.'[41] But at this moment of capitalist crisis, cultural signs are inseparable from a 'shared experience' of insecurity and exploitation, the haunting spectre of the proletarian. This haunting proceeded, in Crane's case, under the material conditions of literary production in the 1890s.

By the early 1890s, the New York newspaper and magazine publishing industry was in the process of installing a 'progressive' managerial system based on 'rationalization, efficiency, and expertise,' a process which had also begun to affect book publishing.[42] At stake in the transformation of publishing by the mass market was the distribution of profits and risks between authors and publishers. Book publishers withheld the payment of royalties until at least a thousand copies had been sold, in effect making the author pay for the costs of production and advertising. Thereafter, the royalty was commonly fixed at 10 percent of the retail price, with a sliding scale of between 15 and 20 percent according to the number of copies sold.[43] The writer fared no better in the quality magazines, where the standard rate during the 1890s for unknown writers was half a cent per word; R. W. Stallman estimates that Crane averaged two or three cents per word over the decade.[44] Publishers and editors were not reticent in referring to themselves as 'procurers of a commodity.'[45] S. S. McClure recalled that, when he founded *McClure's Magazine* in the early 1890s, 'my real capital was my wide acquaintance with writers and with what they could produce.'[46]

According to Marx, to make a profit is to add to one's capital by making the worker perform surplus labour, over and above the labour required to produce the value he receives in wages, wresting from him an additional increment of value which is not returned. The capitalist 'pumps out a certain specific quantum of surplus labour from the direct producers or workers, surplus labour that [he] receives without an equivalent and which by way of its very nature always remains forced labour, however much it might appear as the result of free contractual agreement.'[47] The surplus value produced in the process of exploitation is in fact the 'congealed labour' of the primary producer, which the capitalist consumes as a commodity.[48] This draining of substance from the mind and body of the primary producer is then presented in mystified form as a relation between fetishized objects. 'The magazine and syndicate combined were the machinery I offered to get the young men in whom I believed to the people,' McClure recalls, making the extraction of surplus value merely the incidental means by which the aspirant writer is placed before the admiring eyes of the public.[49]

If Crane suffered from exploitation in the mass market, the material conditions of his existence as a self-styled 'working newspaper man' in the early 1890s were also marked by a proletarian insecurity, despite his ostensibly middle class status as the college-educated son of a Methodist minister.[50] Indeed, it is difficult to tell real from imaginary tatters in the recollections of his friends. After the blizzard which swept New York on the night of 25 February 1894, the artist Corwin Linson found Crane in bed at the Art Students' League building they shared on the Lower East Side, 'haggard' and 'alone.' Crane showed Linson a sketch he just written, 'The Men in the Storm,' the result of a process of arduous labour: '[h]e had been all night at it, out in the storm in line with the hungry men, studying them; then inside, writing it.'[51] When Crane arrived at Hamlin Garland's door in March, 'hungry' and 'seedy,' he told the more established writer in the realist cause that he would trade his 'entire future' for 'twenty-three dollars in cash.'[52] This was roughly the sum needed to redeem the manuscript of *The Red Badge of Courage*, which was in hock to the typist Crane was unable to pay.

Linson recalls that Crane's reaction to his 'voluntary tatters' was indeed the state of 'profound dejection' ascribed to the youth in 'An Experiment in Misery.' But, says Linson, '[h]e actually found relief in the company of genuine bums. And he made a discovery. He said that even if he had not altogether absorbed the tramp's outlook, his own had "undergone a considerable alteration."'[53] Crane's experience in the cheap boarding house was so traumatic that he was compelled to repeat it in fictional form, indicating there was psychic work left to do. But the questions which remain are: how much of the trauma of class can be admitted to consciousness? How far can the identification with the proletarian be allowed go?

III

Henry Fleming in *The Red Badge of Courage* undergoes the same pattern of detached observation mutating into sympathetic identification experienced by the protagonist of 'An Experiment in Misery' (both are referred to as 'the youth'). The key elements in this process appear in the same sequence: an uncanny exchange of looks, prostrate bodies, a scream of protest. The industrial army of 'An Experiment' merges into the army proper of *The Red Badge*, so that reading the novel in sequence with the sketch produces a series of uncanny effects, with wounded soldiers transfigured into distressed proletarians, the squalid spectres walking the land. *The Red Badge of Courage* becomes a 'retroactive working-through,' or 'elaboration' of the repressed 'proletarian' signifier uncovered in 'An Experiment,' a signifier which, like a dream or a symptom, only achieves its full 'symbolic place and meaning' once it has been placed in a new 'signifying frame.'[54]

Henry initially keeps from 'intercourse with his companions' (p. 16). Musing on the 'radical difference' between himself and them, he fails to discover 'any mite of resemblance in their viewpoints' (p. 18). So pronounced is Henry's middle class individualism and his aversion to collective life that as he runs with his comrades in battle he feels 'carried along by a mob' (p. 20). Henry literally disengages himself from his unit by fleeing the battle, carrying 'a dull, animal-like rebellion against his fellows, war in the abstract, and fate' inside him (p. 41). At exactly this point, as Henry enters a 'deep thicke[t],' the staring, 'corpse-like being' from 'An Experiment' returns with its petrifying gaze. Henry finds that he is 'being looked at by a dead man,' seated with his back 'against a column-like tree. The corpse was dressed in a uniform that had once been blue, but was now faded to a melancholy shade of green. The eyes, staring at the youth, had changed to the dull hue to be seen on the side of a dead fish' (p. 43). The uncanny situation of the cheap lodging house is repeated but inverted: it is now a dead man who appears to be living rather than a living man who appears dead. Henry remains 'staring into the liquid-looking eyes,' the two 'exchang[ing] a long look' (p. 43). Just as the corpse-like being at the cheap lodging house lies within reach of the youth's hand, but is untouched by him, Henry feels 'the subtle suggestion' that he should 'touch the corpse,' even as he runs from it: recognition struggling with disavowal (p. 43). He then hears the 'ripping sound of musketry' and runs 'in the direction of the battle' (p. 44). Henry refuses to heed the call of the proletarian other, although he cannot, in the end, escape it.[55]

What happens next transforms Henry's situation via a second return of the repressed. He comes across a man he recognizes, a 'spectral soldier' who is about to die from his wounds (p. 48).

> Something in the gesture of the man as he waved the bloody and pitying soldiers away made the youth start as if bitten. He yelled in horror. Tottering forward he laid a quivering hand upon the man's arm. As the latter slowly turned his waxlike features toward him, the youth screamed:
>
> 'Gawd! Jim Conklin!' (p. 49)

The 'long wails' of the sleeping man in the cheap lodging house, expressive of the plight of the industrial army, are echoed by Henry's scream, which carries with it the mortified recognition that in the proletarian other, returning from the outside, is the image of the self. Henry's denial of his affinity with the proletarian in his weakness and insufficiency is finally overcome, and he is able to lay a quivering hand on the dying man's arm. When Conklin dies—horribly, wretchedly—Henry's face twists 'with an expression of every agony he had imagined for his friend' (p. 52).

Jim Conklin is one of industrial capitalism's walking wounded and, eventually, one of its fatalities; his life substance, to use Marx's metaphor, has been 'pumped out' of him. Henry inspects the corpse:

> He [. . .] sprang to his feet and, going closer, gazed upon the paste-like face. The mouth was open and the teeth showed in a laugh.
>   As the flap of the blue jacket fell away from the body, he could see that the side looked as if it had been chewed by wolves. (p. 52)

This open wound, and the proletarian status it confers, insists on admission to consciousness. Once it has finally broken through, the symbolic necessity is that Henry should acquire his own wound, a wound which represents the repressed trauma of exploitation, the persistence of the proletarian signifier in the middle class unconscious. Henry attempts to rejoin his unit, and receives a blow from the rifle butt of a retreating soldier that gives him the appearance of having engaged in battle, an appearance which helps him gain confidence and plunge into actual conflict. Henry is finally able to wear his proletarian signifier, his red badge of courage.

But the matter is not resolved. The proletarianization of the writer does not mean a final identification with the proletarian. If the wound opens a hole in the fabric of the real which enables the proletarian other to be admitted into consciousness, it also enables that other to be expelled through it, and replaced by another ideal ego: in this case, a young lieutenant.

IV

As Amy Kaplan notes, *The Red Badge of Courage* 'resonates with the tensions' of 'violent class conflicts' between officers and men.[56] The hierarchy of officers—general, colonel, captain, lieutenant—parallels the managerial hierarchy of the modern industrial corporation with its layers of top, middle, and lower managers. Henry's heart is 'continually clamoring' at what he considers to be the 'intolerable slowness of the generals' (13); he is filled with a sense of 'anger at the commanders' (p. 24).

The class divisions between officers and men in *The Red Badge* threaten to cause open conflict when Henry overhears an officer refer to his regiment as 'a lot of mule drivers' who can be safely sacrificed in the battle (p. 89). The officer speaks of the regiment 'as if he referred to a broom' (p. 89). When the men are next ordered to do 'impossible and conflicting things' they 'glowe[r] with bent brows, but dangerously, upon some of the officers' (p. 96). This enmity, however, has the effect of unifying the men and making them work harder to prove themselves. Henry joins the 'savage-minded lieutenant,' who has just silenced his dissent, in a heroic charge, seizing the colours from the mortally wounded bearer, and succeeding with his unit in routing the enemy. Henry feels a greater hatred for the 'cold officer' who has abused the regiment than for the enemy, but he is spurred into an action which leads to his experiencing a feeling of 'subtle fellowship and equality' with the lieutenant (p. 97). Nascent class conflicts are resolved by Henry making a distinction between callous generals, or chief executives, and intermediate officers, or middle managers. The general reproaches the colonel for not carrying on the charge, leaving the men smarting at 'an injustice' (p. 104). But Henry then learns that the colonel has complimented him on his bravery to another officer and his heart fills with 'grateful affection for the colonel and the youthful lieutenant' (p. 105). Henry bears the colours in one final engagement in which he is 'deeply absorbed as a spectator' (p. 108). As he reviews his experience at the close of the novel Henry feels 'gleeful and unregretting,' parading his 'public deeds' in his mind in 'great and shining prominence' (p. 115). He spends 'delightful minutes' viewing 'the gilded images of memory' (p. 115).

Why the change of heart? Why should success in battle lead to 'anger at the commanders' being transmuted into 'grateful affection'? An explanation of a more or less standard psychological kind would no doubt be that Henry has achieved 'maturity,' arriving at an honest estimate of himself and his relation to others, and thereby outgrowing his callow self-absorption and self-doubt.[57] But there is another reading of Henry's *volte face* which involves a further level of allegory in the novel. Henry performs 'public deeds' which are related to 'gilded images'—in other words his success as a soldier is very like success as a writer for the popular market. Indeed, Henry's relation to war has been writerly or literary from the start, where he looks on it as 'some sort of play affair'—if not 'Greeklike struggles,' then 'large pictures extravagant in color, lurid with breathless deeds' (p. 5). In this sense, Henry hasn't travelled very far: from 'large pictures' and 'breathless deeds' to 'public deeds' and 'gilded images' is no great distance, except that he has made himself the protagonist of a 'real' story instead of a purely imaginary one. This is where the most deeply buried layer of allegorical meaning in the novel lies. *The Red Badge of Courage* is the story of a writer attempting to find a place within a corporate system, within, that is to say, the modern publishing business—a writer who succeeds by writing *The Red Badge of Courage*. In trying to find his place, this writer is torn between his newly found identity with tattered men, and the need to furnish saleable products for the generals of industry. It becomes necessary for Crane to again repress the proletarian signifier, or to reattach it to another signifier, that of the writer as middle class hero.

Henry is constantly involved in accumulating 'information of himself,' making 'ceaseless calculations' about the quality of his inner being, his possession of either courage or cowardice (pp. 10, 12). A 'mental outcast,' Henry doesn't know how he will react to combat, and he has plenty of time in the intervals between battles 'to wonder about himself and to attempt to probe his sensations' (p. 22). As Henry prepares for action, a 'thousand details of color and form surg[e] in his mind' (p. 29). Mental activity, sensation and emotion, are here calculable entities which issue in concrete actions with a definite utility: like the raw material of experience which a writer accumulates and converts into written words with a market value. Henry initially hates the lieutenant because he has 'no appreciation of fine minds,' rather as a writer possessed of literary genius might resent an editor who has an eye only for what will sell (p. 23).[58]

Henry has the writer's ambivalence towards words on a page, towards what Michael Fried calls the 'materiality of writing,' which has something deathly about it as the fixed and irrevocable externalization of what has been surging in the mind.[59] Coming across a dead soldier 'staring at the sky,' Henry notices that 'the soles of his shoes had been worn to the thinness of writing paper, and from a great rent in one the dead foot projected piteously' (pp. 21, 22). Shoes and paper are permeable membranes like skin, easily worn out or mutilated. The dead soldier again resembles a tramp, except this time it is the writer who is figured as a worn, expendable figure in the labour process, his paper productions bearing a pitiful vulnerability. The image of paper reappears at Henry's moment of transformation and triumph, when he is able to join what the lieutenant calls the '[h]ot work' of battle without fear. In his inner struggles Henry has 'overcome obstacles which he had admitted to be mountains,' they have 'fallen like paper peaks' (p. 86). Henry is now 'what he called a hero,' even though he has not been 'aware of the process. He had slept and, awakening, found himself a knight' (p. 86). After long being 'frustrated by hateful circumstances,' the accumulation of experience and the performance of the task have finally paid off. Henry wakes to find himself honoured and famous, the fulfillment of every writer's dream.

This, of course, is what happened to Crane. The thousand surging details of colour and form were applauded as 'psychological realism' or 'literary impressionism' by a host of British and American critics eager to hail Crane's artistry, and, at the same time, to detach it from any pressing social context. The novel was received as 'an extraordinary and merciless realization of the psychology of combat;' a 'record of impressions [...] of a vigor and intensity beyond all precedent.'[60] The image of Crane as an apolitical stylist is an enduring one, from Alfred Kazin's assertion that Crane was 'never troubled' by the depression of the 1890s, and 'cared not a jot which way the world went,' to Stanley Wertheim and Paul Sorrentino's judgement that, despite his 'empathy with social outcasts,' Crane 'never formulated convictions about the causes of social injustice.'[61]

But the text cannot shake itself free of its own context as easily as this. Still, at the close of *The Red Badge of Courage*, there 'loom[s]' in Henry's mind 'the dogging memory of the tattered soldier,' a memory which causes him to 'blus[h]' (p. 115). The tattered soldier 'gored by bullets and faint for blood,' had 'fretted' over Henry's 'imagined wound,' had 'loaned the last of his strength and intellect for the tall solider,' only to be 'deserted in the field' by Henry (p. 115). Henry has been so self-absorbed and fearful as to be incapable of comradeship and self-sacrifice. Crane perceived the conflict between individual aspiration and human solidarity in a like manner—a conflict all the more pressing since he has come to recognize the affinities between the soldier in the industrial army and the writer in the mass market. If we give full credence to this residue of class feeling in the novel, to the 'sombre phantom' of the 'desertion in the field,' and to Jim Conklin's 'stalking reproach,' then there is less credence to be given to Henry's 'conviction' that his past self is unlike his present self, or to the 'store of assurance' this brings (pp. 116, 48, 116). If Henry worries about selling out his comrades in the pursuit of 'public deeds' and 'gilded images,' then perhaps it is appropriate that Crane should have left his editor, Ripley Hitchcock, to mutilate his manuscript by cutting down the satire of Henry and boosting the feel-good factor of the ending ('[o]ver the river a golden ray of sun came through the hosts of leaden gray clouds' [p. 117]).[62] Now that the war of industrial consolidation is under way, the writer will have to place his or her 'store of assurance' in the vagaries and derangements of the mass market. In the struggle against imminent proletarianization in the era of corporate capital, who dares wear the red badge of class?

NOTES

1. David A. Wells, *Recent Economic Changes and Their Effect on the Production and Distribution of Wealth and the Well-Being of Society* (London, 1890), p. vi.
2. *Ibid.*, p. 72.
3. *Ibid.*
4. *Ibid.*, p. 80.

5. Martin J. Sklar, *The Corporate Reconstruction of American Capitalism, 1890–1916: The Market, the Law, and Politics* (Cambridge, 1988), p. 43. On the 'chronic state or perturbation' characteristic of advanced industrial capitalism, see Thorstein Veblen, *The Theory of Business Enterprise* (New York, 1904), pp. 20–65, esp. p. 34. On 'overproduction' as a symptom of the new economic order, see Wells, *Recent Economic Changes*, pp. 70–114; Joseph Dorfman, *The Economic Mind in American Civilisation, Vol. 3, 1865–1918* (1949, rpt. New York, 1969), pp. 130–36; Sklar, *Corporate Reconstruction*, 43–85. See also Ian McGuire, 'W. D. Howells and the Crisis of Reproduction,' *Journal of American Studies* 33:3 (1999), 459–472.

6. Amy Kaplan, 'The Spectacle of War in Crane's Revision of History,' in Lee Clark Mitchell, ed., *New Essays on 'The Red Badge of Courage'* (Cambridge, 1986), p. 92, p. 91.

7. Donald Pizer, '*The Red Badge of Courage*: Text, Theme, and Form,' Southern Atlantic Quarterly, 84 (1985), 308.

8. Stephen Crane, *The Red Badge of Courage and Other Stories*, eds Anthony Mellors and Fiona Robertson (Oxford, 1998), p. 82. Subsequent references to this edition will be made in parentheses, in the text.

9. For the dating of the manuscript, see R. W. Stallman, *Stephen Crane: A Biography* (New York, 1973), p. 72; p. 92.

10. Sklar, *Corporate Reconstruction*, p. 5.

11. R. Hal Williams, *Years of Decision: American Politics in the 1890s* (New York, 1978), p. 76; see also Charles Hoffman, *The Depression of the Nineties: An Economic History* (Westport, Conn., 1970), pp. 47–96.

12. See Harold U. Faulkner, *Politics, Reform, and Expansion 1890–1900* (London, 1959), pp. 141–162.

13. Samuel Rezneck, 'Unemployment, Unrest, and Relief in the United States During the Depression of 1893–97,' *Journal of Political Economy*, 61 (1953), p. 328.

14. Quoted in Rezneck, 'Unemployment, Unrest, and Relief,' p. 329.

15. William Dean Howells, 'Are We a Plutocracy?' *North American Review*, 158: 447 (1894), 194.

16. Carlos Schwantes, *Coxey's Army: An American Odyssey* (Lincoln, Nebraska, 1985), p. 42. See also Philip S. Foner, *History of the Labor Movement in the United States, Vol 2: From the Founding of the American Federation of Labor to the Emergence of American Imperialism* (New York, 1955), pp. 241–43.

17. *Ibid.*, p. 6.

18. Thomas Byrnes, 'The Menace of Coxeyism, II: Character and Methods of the Men,' *North American Review*, 158:451 (June 1894), p. 700.

19. W. T. McCulloch to Ignatius Donnelly, in *The Populist Mind*, ed. Norman Pollack (Indianapolis, 1967), p. 35.

20. Quoted in James Edward Wright, *The Politics of Populism: Dissent in Colorado* (New Haven, 1974), p. 170.

21. Samuel Gompers, 'Organized Labor in the Campaign,' *North American Review*, 155:428 (July 1892), p. 93.

22. Chester McArthur Destler, *American Radicalism 1865–1901: Essays and Documents* (New London, Conn., 1946), p. 20. See also Richard Hofstadter, *The Age of Reform: From Bryan to F. D. R.* (1955, rpt. New York, 1968), pp. 36–46; Hofstadter, 'North America' in *Populism: Its Meaning and National Characteristics*, eds Ghita Ionescu and Ernest Gellner (Macmillan, 1969), pp. 9–27. The view that the Populist cause had little or no appeal to industrial workers is advanced by, among

others, Lawrence Goodwyn, *Democratic Promise: The Populist Moment in America* (New York, 1976), pp. 309–310; Alan Trachtenberg, *The Incorporation of America: Culture and Society in the Gilded Age* (New York, 1982), pp. 176–77. For a recent assessment which emphasizes the subordinate role of labour in Populist reform, see Elizabeth Sanders, *Roots of Reform: Farmers, Workers, and the American State 1877–1917* (Chicago, 1999).

23. Farmers' Alliance resolution, Kansas *Advocate*, 27 July 1892, quoted in Norman Pollack, *The Populist Response to Industrial America: Midwestern Populist Thought* (Cambridge, Mass., 1962), p. 48. See also Pollack, ed., *The Populist Mind*, which collects Populist documents on the degradation of labour, monopoly capitalism, and support for the unemployed.

24. Wright, *Politics of Populism*, p. 169. Destler shows how Populism momentarily provided a unifying force for a fragmented labour movement in the Midwest, resulting in the long desired 'consummation' of a Populist-labour alliance in Illinois; see *American Radicalism*, pp. 162–211. On the support of Kansas and Iowa Populists for the industrial armies, see John D. Hicks, *The Populist Revolt: A History of the Farmers' Alliance and the People's Party* (1931, rpt. Lincoln, 1961), pp. 323–24.

25. Quoted in Foner, *History of the Labor Movement*, p. 242.

26. Paul Buhle, *Marxism in the United States: Remapping the History of the American Left*, rev. ed. (London, 1991), p. 50; p. 51. See also Gerald Grob, *Workers and Utopia: A Study of Ideological Conflict in the American Labor Movement 1865–1900* (Evanston, Ill., 1961), pp. 167–171.

27. Henry Vincent, *The Story of the Commonwealth* (1894, rpt. New York, 1969), pp. 14–15.

28. *Ibid.*, p. 18.

29. See Karl Marx, *Capital, Vol 1*, trans. Ben Fowkes (Harmondsworth, 1976), pp. 781–94.

30. Corwin Knapp Linson, *My Stephen Crane* (Syracuse, 1958), p. 62.

31. Fredson Bowers, ed., *The Works of Stephen Crane, Volume 8: Tales, Sketches, and Reports* (Charlottesville, 1973), p. 862. Further references are given in parentheses in the text.

32. Sigmund Freud, 'The Uncanny,' *Standard Edition of the Complete Psychological Works of Sigmund Freud*, Volume 27, ed. James Strachey (London, 1955), p. 226.

33. *Ibid.*, p. 241.

34. *Ibid.*, p. 236.

35. Quoted in Wai-Chee Dimock, *Empire for Liberty: Melville and the Poetics of Individualism* (Princeton, 1991), p. 19.

36. Karl Marx, *The Poverty of Philosophy* (New York, 1963 [1847]), p. 173.

37. Eric Schocket, 'Undercover Explorations of the "Other Half," Or the Writer as Class Transvestite,' *Representations*, 64 (Fall 1998), p. 121.

38. Louis J. Budd, 'The American Background,' *The Cambridge Companion to American Realism and Naturalism: Howells to London* (Cambridge, 1995), p. 42.

39. Schocket, 'Undercover Explorations,' pp. 113–14. In *Self-Rule: A Cultural History of American Democracy* (Chicago, 1995), Robert H. Wiebe usefully describes how the 'permeable boundary between classes' (114) became, in late nineteenth century America, a 'giant slide [...] pushing more and more people into the class borderland' (121). On the slippery border between middle and lower classes in particular, see also Paul T. Ringenbach, *Tramps and Reformers 1873–1916: The Discovery of Unemployment in New York* (Westport, Conn., 1973), pp. 36–81.

40. Quoted in Pollack, *Populist Response*, p. 36.

41. Schocket, 'Undercover Explorations,' p. 120.

42. Christopher P. Wilson, *The Labor of Words: Literary Professionalism in the Progressive Era* (Athens, Georgia, 1985), p. 19.

43. John Tebbel, *A History of Book Publishing in the United States, Vol. 2: The Expansion of an Industry 1865–1919* (New York, 1975), 15; see also 130–149. On progressive publishing, see also Daniel H. Borus, *Writing Realism: Howells, James, and Norris in the Mass Market* (Chapel Hill, 1989), 27–64; Wilson, *Labor of Words*, 40–91.

44. Stallman, *Stephen Crane*, p. 400 n.9. Writing for the mass market thus resembles industrial piece-work, which as Marx notes, is 'the most fruitful source of reductions in wages, and of frauds committed by the capitalists' (*Capital, Vol. 1*, p. 694).

45. Borus, *Writing Realism*, p. 42.

46. S. S. McClure, *My Autobiography* (1914, rpt. New York, 1963), p. 234.

47. Karl Marx, *Capital: A Critique of Political Economy, Volume 3*, trans. David Fernbach (Harmondsworth, 1981), p. 958. On Marx's account of exploitation, see Richard J. Arneson, 'What's Wrong With Exploitation?' *Ethics* 91:2 (January 1981), 202–227; Norman Geras, 'The Controversy About Marx and Justice,' *New Left Review* 150 (March/April 1985), 47–88; Etienne Balibar, *Masses, Classes, Ideas: Studies on Politics and Philosophy Before and After Marx*, trans. James Swenson (New York, 1994), pp. 125–149.

48. Frederick Engels, 'Preface,' to Karl Marx, *Capital: A Critique of Political Economy, Volume 2*, trans. David Fernbach (Harmondsworth, 1978), p. 99.

49. McClure, *My Autobiography*, p. 235.

50. The designation is attributed to Crane by William Macintosh, 'The Philistines at Dinner,' *Buffalo Evening News* (20 December 1895), quoted in Stanley Wertheim and Paul Sorrentino, *The Crane Log: A Documentary Life of Stephen Crane 1871–1900* (New York, 1994), p. 156. On Crane's class background and upbringing see Stallman, *Stephen Crane*, pp. 1–6.

51. Linson, 'Little Stories of "Steve" Crane,' *Saturday Evening Post* 175 (11 April 1903), quoted in *ibid.*, p. 97.

52. Hamlin Garland, *Roadside Meetings* (St. Clair Shores, Michigan, 1977), p. 198.

53. Corwin Knap Linson, *My Stephen Crane*, p. 61.

54. Slavoj Zizek, *The Sublime Object of Ideology* (London, 1989), p. 56.

55. For a different reading, see Terry Mulcaire, in 'Progressive Visions of War in *The Red Badge of Courage* and *The Principles of Scientific Management*,' *American Quarterly*, 43:1 (1991), 46–72. Mulcaire first argues that Henry is committed to 'a martial form of rational, industrial efficiency,' and then identifies the staring corpse with both 'an uncanny scientific manager' and 'incorrigibly lazy' workers (59; 63) in order to position Crane as a critic of 'disinterested' spectatorship (64). This seems to me to elide vital questions of class position and interest raised by the parallel structures of *The Red Badge* and 'An Experiment in Misery.' For a claim similar to that of Mulcaire, that Crane's concern is with 'the moral deficiency of spectatorship,' see Andrew Delbanco, 'The American Stephen Crane: The Context of *The Red Badge of Courage*,' *New Essays on 'The Red Badge of Courage*,' ed. Lee Clark Mitchell (Cambridge, 1986), pp. 49–76, esp. p. 67.

56. Amy Kaplan, 'The Spectacle of War in Crane's Revision of History,' *New Essays on 'The Red Badge of Courage,'* p. 88.

57. See, for example Sidney Brooks, *Saturday Evening Post* (11 January 1896), in Richard M. Weatherford, ed., *Stephen Crane: The Critical Heritage* (London, 1973), pp. 99–103; Eric Solomon, S*tephen Crane: From Parody to Realism* (Cambridge, Mass., 1967), pp. 82, 87, 97.

58. On the commodification of raw 'experience' by mass market magazine and book publishing, see Christopher P. Wilson, *The Labor of Words: Literary Professionalism in the Progressive Era* (Athens, Georgia, 1985), pp. 40–91, esp. p. 89.

59. Michael Fried, *Realism, Writing, Disfiguration: On Thomas Eakins and Stephen Crane* (Chicago, 1987), p. 132.

60. Anon., New York *Press* (13 October, 1895), Weatherford, *Critical Heritage*, 86; H. G. Wells (*North American Review*, August 1900), *ibid.*, p. 274. See also Robert Wooster, *Stephen Crane: An Omnibus* (New York, 1953), p. 185; Rodney O. Rogers, 'Stephen Crane and Impressionism' in Thomas A. Gullason ed., *Stephen Crane's Career: Perspectives and Evaluations* (New York, 1972), pp. 264–77; James Nagel, *Stephen Crane and Literary Impressionism* (University Park, Pa., 1980).

61. Alfred Kazin, *On Native Grounds: An Interpretation of Modern American Prose Literature* (New York, 1942), p. 67; p. 68. Wertheim and Sorrentino, *Correspondence*, p. 42.

62. On Hitchcock's revisions, see Hershel Parker, 'Getting Used to the "Original Form" of *The Red Badge of Courage*,' in Mitchell, *New Essays*, pp. 25–47.

MICHAEL SCHAEFER

"Heroes Had No Shame in Their Lives": Manhood, Heroics, and Compassion in The Red Badge of Courage and "A Mystery of Heroism"

The Civil War, the bloodiest conflict ever conducted on American soil, raged for four years. Far longer, though fortunately less bloody, at least in literal terms, has been the conflict over the meaning of the greatest novel of that war, Stephen Crane's *The Red Badge of Courage*. The central issue in this debate is whether Crane intends for the reader to take the protagonist's final assessment of himself straightforwardly or ironically. On his first day of battle, Henry Fleming flees in terror and endures various physical and mental agonies as a result, including being clubbed in the head by another panic-stricken man and fearing that his cowardice will be revealed to all, to his undying shame. However, upon returning to his unit that evening, Fleming finds his comrades willing to accept his lie that he was "separated" from them during the fighting and that his head wound was caused by enemy fire. Realizing that he "had performed his mistakes in the dark, so he was still a man" (86), Fleming fights fiercely the next day, winning praise from his officers and fellow soldiers. With these plaudits ringing in his ears, he concludes that he is "now what he called a hero" (97) and, indeed, as he had concluded earlier, "a man" (135). John J. McDermott is representative of the critics who argue that Crane wishes for the reader likewise to call Henry a hero and a man, discerning in Henry's deeds on the second day "a final pattern of courageous action" and thus "genuine heroics" (330). Weihong

From *War, Literature, and the Arts* 18, nos. 1–2 (2006): 104–13. Copyright © 2006 by Michael Schaefer.

Julia Zhu, on the other hand, offers one of the most recent statements of the opposing view, asserting that Henry's courage is "absurd" on several counts.[1] My own view, based on a close reading of *The Red Badge* that synthesizes the separate insights of a number of other critics, and on the depiction of heroics and manhood that Crane offers in "A Mystery of Heroism," the first Civil War story he wrote after this novel, is that the ironic interpretation is accurate but no single critic has probed the full depths of Crane's interrogation of these subjects.

Most of the negative critiques of Henry's self-assessment examine the nature of the courage he displays. Howard Horsford argues that Henry's supposed bravery on the second day is finally no different from his flight on the first in that neither behavior stems from "conscious, willed intention"; his flight results from fear, while his courage results from an equally involuntary upwelling of the opposite emotion, rage (123). As John Clendenning more elaborately explains, "Henry's shameful cowardice, his archaic dependence on motherly solicitation—the specter of a primitive female identification—his fear, in short, that he is not a real man and others know it, turns to furious hatred" on the second day. He "now wants to destroy the enemy whom he perceives as somehow to be blamed for his impotence. His rage—or what self psychologist Heinz Kohut calls 'narcissistic rage'—is his revenge against everyone and everything that insults his grandiose, exhibitionist self" (31). Picking up on the note of narcissism, Zhu rates Henry's courage as absurd partly on the grounds that it "derives from vanity"—from his desire to gain the praise of his peers and superiors—rather than from the "righteous inducement" of true mental or moral force (3–4).

Support for these views is widespread in Crane's depiction of Henry's second day of battle. That Henry operates out of vanity, judging himself only on the basis of what others can see rather than his own moral sense, is clear both before and after the fighting. Early in the morning, while Henry is waiting for marching orders, we are told that "since [he knew that] nothing could now be discovered" about his cowardice, he "did not shrink from the eyes of judges, and allowed no thoughts of his own to keep him from an attitude of manfulness" (86). Similarly, when the fighting is over Henry is said to feel "gleeful and unregretting, for, in it, his public deeds were paraded in great and shining prominence. Those performances which had been witnessed by his fellows marched now in wide purple and gold, hiding various deflections" (133).

That Henry's prime motivation under fire is unconscious anger comes across most sharply in the account of the first combat of this day. The narrator says that "When, in a dream, it occurred to the youth that his rifle was an impotent stick, he lost sense of everything but his hate, his desire to smash into pulp the glittering smile of victory which he could feel upon the faces of his enemies . . . The youth was not conscious that he was erect upon his feet. He did not know the direction of the ground" (95). So all-consuming is this rage that Henry is not even aware that the enemy has retreated until someone from his own side forcibly points the fact out, at which time "there appeared upon the glazed vacancy of his eyes, a diamond-point of intelligence" (96). Even in a later moment when Henry might seem to perform a conscious act of unselfish heroism, recklessly exposing himself to enemy fire in an effort to rally his regiment when it has stalled during a charge, vanity and rage are the true engines, for his goal in this endeavor is to prove wrong the officer who earlier predicted just this outcome in saying that the regiment fights "'like a lot 'a mule-drivers'" (101). Specifically, Henry wishes to prove that *he* is no mule-driver, as the description of his thoughts at this moment reveals. We are told that "a scowl of mortification and rage was upon his face . . . His dreams had collapsed when the mule-drivers, dwindling rapidly, had wavered and hesitated on the little clearing and then had recoiled. And now the retreat of the mule-drivers was a march of shame to him" (111).

Despite the seemingly condemnatory nature of such passages, a number of critics have suggested that negative judgment of Henry on the bases of anger and vanity is contained in the minds of readers operating out of certain twentieth century paradigms of courage rather than in the text itself. Philip Beidler argues that the reader must be aware of nineteenth-century concepts of heroism, both romantic and Darwinian, out of which Crane is writing. When Henry's thoughts and actions are viewed in the context of the contemporary "discourse of courage," Beidler says, it is possible, while not disregarding a great deal of complexity, to conclude that, for Crane,

> Henry has proven commonly battleworthy by common definition, and specifically that he is as courageous as he or anyone else might expect to be . . . Whether he is deluded or not *is* an issue and the focus throughout of a complex irony, but it is only so within this very specific context. He has simply been one of those left alive and accredited in the consensus of his fellows—and thus also in cultural memory—as having met the test. (250)

And even within twentieth-century discourses of courage Henry's behavior may be regarded as normative rather than deficient. John Hersey concludes, on the basis of his observation of a marine unit's combat experience on Guadalcanal in 1942, that "except for the hard knot which is inside some men, courage is largely the desire to show other men that you have it" (qtd. in Monteiro, "Guadalcanal Report" 199–200). Tim O'Brien offers much the same assessment of men in Vietnam in *The Things They Carried*. Among those things, he says, is "the soldier's greatest fear, which was the fear of blushing. Men killed, and died, because they were embarrassed not to" (20–21).

One critical response to this less judgmental measure of Henry's courage has been to sever the connection Henry himself makes between heroism and manhood. Donald Pizer says that Henry's bravery on the second day does not differ in substance from his fear on the first "in their essential character as animal and instinctive responses to danger" (2), but he argues that Henry's experiences have run him through the whole gamut of human emotions and have thereby conferred some measure of growth upon him. "To have touched the great death as Henry has done," Pizer concludes, "and to have experienced as well the central emotions of life arising from this inescapable reality of the human condition, is indeed to have . . . gained some degree of manhood" (6–7).

This is a sensitive and intelligent reading, one that takes into account the uncertain relationship between courage and maturity, but I would argue, as do a number of other critics, that it does not take into account Henry's lack of one emotion that for Crane is central to both manhood and heroism: compassion. In a letter dated January 12, 1896, just months after the publication of *The Red Badge*, Crane explained his view on this matter to Nellie Crouse, a young woman with whom he was enamored. "The final wall of the wise man's thought," he says, "is Human Kindness of course. If the road of disappointment, grief, pessimism, is followed far enough, it will arrive there . . . Therefore do I strive to be as kind and as just as may be to those about me and in my meager success at it, I find the solitary pleasure of life" (*Correspondence* 180). It might be tempting to dismiss such a statement in such a context as youthful self-dramatization, but, as Crane says in the same letter, "[t]he cynical mind is an uneducated thing" (180), and *The Red Badge* bears out the philosophy of the letter, for Crane seems clearly to show that Henry is at fault for deriving his pleasure in life from other sources while consciously refusing to act out of human kindness.

The most glaring example of Henry's failure in this area spans both days of battle. Shortly after his flight on the first day, as he wanders behind the lines, Henry falls in with a column of wounded men, among whom he finds one of his best friends, Jim Conklin. Near death, Conklin asks Henry to keep him out of the road so he will not be run over by "'them damned artillery wagons'" (55). Henry responds, "hysterically," by the narrator's description, "'I'll take care of you! I swear to Gawd I will'" (55). Henry at this moment clearly does feel compassion, but the adverb *hysterically* suggests that this response may be, like his fear and courage, not entirely a matter of conscious will. When he is presented with a chance to show a more considered compassion a few moments later, he fails utterly. Following Conklin's death, another mortally wounded man who has befriended Henry shows solicitude for him, asking him where he has been wounded. Lacking a wound, Henry is afraid that this question will reveal that he is only behind the lines because he ran from the battle. As a result, he is "enraged against the tattered man and could have strangled him;" despite the man's entreaties that Henry stay with him, Henry walks away, leaving him "wandering about helplessly in the fields" (62).

At the end of the next day, as Henry is gleefully surveying his public deeds of courage, he recalls this man who displayed compassion and received none in return—"he who gored by bullets and faint for blood, had fretted concerning an imagined wound in another . . . he who blind with weariness and pain had been deserted in the field" (134)—and the memory depresses him. This feeling does not proceed from any deep moral regret, however, but rather from "the thought that he might be detected in the thing" (134). In this new mood he fears that his comrades are "seeing his thoughts and scrutinizing each detail of the scene with the tattered soldier," but, as was the case with his flight on the first day, as soon as he realizes that this mistake too was performed in the dark his remorse vanishes. "[G]radually," the narrator says, "he mustered force to put the sin at a distance" and is able to conclude that "[h]e had been to touch the great death and found that, after all, it was but the great death. He was a man" (135).

However complicated Crane may make the relationship of courage to manhood, the irony in this juxtaposition of compassion and manhood seems clear: when Henry in fact confronted the great death in the form of the tattered soldier, he consciously *refused* to touch it, and so his assessment of himself is of by precisely 180 degrees. Pizer takes account of this flaw and acknowledges that it militates against Henry's having attained complete maturity, but further evidence suggests that compassion is a *sine qua non* of any sort of maturity for Crane and that he equally "conceives of humanity in heroism" (Zhu 6); for, as Zhu, Kevin J. Hayes, and Mary Neff Shaw have all noted, Henry's treatment of the tattered man is not an isolated episode but rather part of a pattern designed to show that Henry consistently behaves with "inhuman selfishness" (Zhu 6).[2] When Henry returns to his unit at the end of the first day with his story of separation and wounding, he is tended by his friend Wilson, who earlier had been boastful and quarrelsome but has been changed by his experiences under fire into the soul of compassion. He gives Henry his own canteen, dresses his wound, and puts him to bed in his own blankets. Henry is grateful, concluding that Wilson has "now climbed a peak of wisdom from which he could perceive himself as a very wee thing" (82), but he does not apply this analysis to himself and deal with Wilson in kind. Rather, when he fears that Wilson, like the tattered soldier, may

unwittingly ask questions that will expose his cowardice, he recalls his knowledge of Wilson's own earlier fears, the tangible evidence of which is a packet
of letters Wilson gave Henry, and "rejoice[s] in the possession of a small
weapon with which he could prostrate his comrade at the first signs of a
cross-examination. He was master. It would now be he who could laugh and
shoot the shafts of derision" (85). Less developed but equally telling is Henry's
behavior toward wounded men on the second day. Twice Henry encounters
badly shot-up comrades, one "thrashing about in the grass, twisting his body
into many strange postures [and] ... screaming loudly" (99) and the other
with his mouth pulped into "a pulsing mass of blood and teeth" (125–26),
but in neither case does the vividness of his observation seem to evoke any
sympathy for them; he merely notes their sufferings and moves along, intent
on his own battle-fury.

It is this lack of compassion for the wounded that provides the link in
terms of both plot and ideology to the short story "A Mystery of Heroism."
Here Crane creates an equal number of significant parallels to and differences
from the novel. Like Henry Fleming, Private Fred Collins, the protagonist
of "Mystery," behaves bravely out of concern for the opinion of others, and
like Henry he faces a challenge to act with compassion that entails personal
risk in the face of the great death. Unlike Henry, however, Collins is capable
of honest introspection and is therefore less sure of his own status as a man
and a hero even though he passes the test of compassion as well as that of
courage; and it would seem that his uncertainty provides a clear intertextual
criticism of Henry.

The test of courage begins for Collins when, as his company is deployed
at the edge of a meadow that is being shelled by Confederate artillery, he
repeatedly complains of thirst and expresses a desire to drink from a well on
the opposite side of the meadow. His comrades' reaction is to ask, "'Well, if
yeh want a drink so bad, why don't yeh go git it?'" (50), which raises Collins's
hackles. Before he fully realizes what he is doing, he takes the dare and asks
his captain's and colonel's permission to make the hazardous run across the
meadow. Although these officers deem his expedition foolhardy, they grant
his request on condition that he take some other men's canteens with him,
thus giving his action some semblance of purpose. At this point Collins's
meditation on heroism begins. Unlike Henry prior to his first battle, he is
not worried about fear; in fact, he feels none and wonders at this circumstance "because human expression had said loudly for centuries that men
should feel afraid of certain things and that all men who did not feel this fear
were phenomena, heroes" (53). Given this line of reasoning, Collins has no
choice but to conclude that "[h]e was, then, a hero," but, again unlike Henry,
he is not elated by this realization. Instead, we are told, "[h]e suffered that

disappointment which we would all have"—all, apparently, but Henry—"if we discovered that we were ourselves capable of those deeds which we most admire in history and legend. This, then, was a hero. After all, heroes were not much" (53).

As downbeat as this induction is, Collins's meditation does not end here; rather, Crane has him descend from even this disheartening level. Collins finally decides that he is not a hero after all, for

> Heroes had no shame in their lives and, as for him, he remembered borrowing fifteen dollars from a friend and promising to pay it back the next day, and then avoiding that friend for ten months. When at home his mother had aroused him for the early labor of his life on the farm, it had often been his fashion to be irritable, childish, diabolical, and his mother had died since he had come to the war. (53)

Once more, the distance between Henry and Collins is sharp: whereas Henry leaves compassion out of his definition of his own heroism in putting "at a distance" his own "sin" of abandoning the tattered man, Collins feels that his significantly lesser failures to consider the needs of others render him "an intruder in the land of fine deeds" (53).

Collins's reflections end at this point, for once he begins his run across the meadow he has no time for introspection. Now, with shells exploding all around him, he does feel fear, but instead of wondering how this new access of emotion might affect his conception of himself, he is concerned only with getting out of jeopardy as fast as possible. Exasperated at how slowly the first canteen fills, he tosses aside all the canteens, instead fills a bucket he finds at the well, and begins the dash back to his own lines with that vessel. Then, out on the meadow, he encounters a mortally wounded Union officer pinned beneath his dead horse. In agony, the officer asks, "'Say, young man, give me a drink of water, can't you?'" (55). Collins, "mad from the threats of destruction," screams, "'I can't'" and continues running (55). An instant later, however, he turns, comes back, and, despite his continuing terror, attempts to succor the officer, who, with "the faintest shadow of a smile on his lips," gives "a sigh, a little primitive breath like that of a child" (56) even though all the trembling Collins can do for him is splash water on his face before dashing away again. In another moment, Collins reaches his regiment, his comrades cheer him—not, it would seem, for his small act of compassion but rather for the grand, foolhardy gesture of running the enemy's gauntlet—and the story ends by living up to its title: where at the end of *The Red Badge* we are treated to Henry's lengthy post-combat analysis of himself, here we know nothing about what conclusion Collins reaches regarding his experience; all we learn is that "two genial, sky-larking young lieutenants" wrestle playfully for the bucket until "[s]uddenly there was an oath, the thud of wood on the ground, and a swift murmur of astonishment from the ranks. The two lieutenants glared at each other. The bucket lay on the ground empty" (56).

Faced with this enigma, critics have wrestled as well, if less playfully than the lieutenants. Thomas Gullason sees this last image as Crane's final word on the mystery, asserting that "Collins's journey ... invalidates the age-old notions regarding the meaning and value of heroism ... The empty bucket sounds and resounds with aftereffects—of the praise lavished upon Collins by his fellow troopers, and the hollowness of his feat, with Collins graceless under pressure, where pride, panic, and group pressure have 'conspired' to make him an 'accidental' hero" (188). Similarly, George Monteiro says that "the irony [of the empty bucket] is unmistakable. Collins has risked his life for nothing. His heroics have gone for naught" (69). These are insightful and trenchant readings, but I would argue that in their focus on the end of the story they ignore the possible import of Collins's compassion for the wounded officer. My own view inclines more to those of Mary Neff Shaw and Patrick Dooley, who give attention to the final image of the bucket but also take heed of Collins's act of charity when the bucket still contains water. Shaw perceives a satiric opposition between the dash across the meadow and the moment of compassion, arguing that the former embodies "a superficial, self-centered attitude ... that heroism is determined by social acclaim" and that the latter demonstrates that "[t]he primary constituent of Crane's personal concept of heroism is human kindness" (97). Dooley goes so far as to brand Collins's dash "immoral" because of the great disparity between its "serious cost and ... trivial reward"; by contrast, Collins's giving water to the officer makes the point that "pain and suffering correctly appreciated by both the patient and the onlooker—and correctly responded to—[can transform] a foolish caper into a genuinely moral act of heroism" (125).

My affinity for these latter two readings is rooted in the fact that they take in more of the story than the first two, but even these two overlook still another mystery of heroism. Shaw and Dooley evidently assume that Collins's return to the officer is a conscious, willed act, but our lack of access to Collins's thoughts once he begins his race means that we cannot be sure this is the case. We are told only that he first runs past the officer and then comes back; we are not told what mental process, if any, has impelled this turnabout. Monteiro asserts that the return is in fact involuntary and that Crane thus "brushes aside the notion that heroism is an act of the will or intention" (69). I am not willing to go this far, but I concur with Monteiro's final assessment that this story "questions the notion that heroism can be defined essentially—which may be Crane's key to the mysteries of heroism" (70). Indeed, I would argue that when we read *The Red Badge of Courage* in the light of this story and vice versa Crane confronts us with not one but at least four mysteries of heroism: why men such as Henry Fleming and Fred Collins are willing to risk their lives for the sake of vanity, where the courage to perform a truly selfless act comes from, how Fleming can possibly regard himself as a hero, and how Collins can fail to do so.

Notes

1. For other discussions of this controversy, see Harold Beaver, "Stephen Crane: The Hero as Victim," *Yearbook of English Studies* 12 (1982): 186–93; Christine Brooke-Rose, "Ill Logics of Irony," *New Essays on The Red Badge of Courage*, ed. Lee Clark Mitchell (Cambridge: Cambridge UP, 1986), 129–46; John J. Conder, "*The Red Badge of Courage*: Form and Function," *Modern American Fiction: Form and Function*, Ed. Thomas Daniel Young (Baton Rouge: Louisiana State UP, 1989), 28–38; John Fraser, "Crime and Forgiveness: '*The Red Badge*' in Time of War," *Criticism* 9 (1967): 243–56; Leland Krauth, "Heroes and Heroics: Stephen Crane's Moral Imperative," *South Dakota Review* 11 (1973): 86–93; Wayne Charles Miller, "A New Kind of War Demands a New Kind of Treatment: The Civil War and the Birth of American Realism," *An Armed America, Its Face in Fiction: A History of the American Military Novel* (New York: New York UP, 1970), 58–91; Donald Pizer, "Late Nineteenth-Century American Naturalism," *Realism and Naturalism in Nineteenth-Century American Literature* (Carbondale: Southern Illinois UP, 1966), 11–32; Kermit Vanderbilt and Daniel Weiss, "From Rifleman to Flagbearer: Henry Fleming's Separate Peace in *The Red Badge of Courage*," *Modern Fiction Studies* 11 (1966): 371–80; Daniel Weiss, "*The Red Badge of Courage*," *Psychoanalytic Review* 52 (1965): 176–96, 460–84.

2. See Hayes's "How Stephen Crane Shaped Henry Fleming," *Studies in the Novel* 22 (1990): 296–307; and Shaw's "Henry Fleming's Heroics in *The Red Badge of Courage*: A Satiric Search for a 'Kinder, Gentler' Heroism," *Studies in the Novel* 22 (1990): 418–28.

Works Cited

Beidler, Philip D. "Stephen Crane's *The Red Badge of Courage*: Henry Fleming's Courage in Its Contexts." *CLIO* 20 (1991): 235–51.

Clendenning, John. "Visions of War and Versions of Manhood." *Stephen Crane in War and Peace: A Special Edition of War, Literature & the Arts* (1999): 23–34.

Crane, Stephen. "A Mystery of Heroism." *Tales of War. Vol. VI, The Works of Stephen Crane*. Ed. Fredson Bowers. Charlottesville: U of Virginia P, 1970. 48–56.

———. *The Red Badge of Courage*. Vol. II, *The Works of Stephen Crane*. Ed. Fredson Bowers. Charlottesville, VA: U of Virginia P, 1975.

Dooley, Patrick. "'A Wound Gives Strange Dignity to Him Who Bears It': Stephen Crane's Metaphysics of Experience." *Stephen Crane in War and Peace: A Special Edition of War, Literature & the Arts* (1999): 116–27.

Gullason, Thomas. "Modern Pictures of War in Stephen Crane's Short Stories." *Stephen Crane in War and Peace: A Special Edition of War, Literature & the Arts* (1999): 183–96.

Horsford, Howard C. "He Was a Man." *New Essays on The Red Badge of Courage.* Ed. Lee
    Clark Mitchell. Cambridge: Cambridge UP, 1986. 109–27.

McDermott, John J. "Symbolism and Psychological Realism in *The Red Badge of Courage.*"
    Nineteenth-Century Fiction 23 (1968): 324–31.

Monteiro, George. "After *The Red Badge*: Mysteries of Heroism, Death, and Burial in Ste-
    phen Crane's Fiction." *American Literary Realism* 28 (1995): 66–79.

———. "John Hersey's Guadalcanal Report: Drawing on Crane's War." *Stephen Crane in War
    and Peace: A Special Edition of War, Literature & the Arts* (1999): 197–208.

O'Brien, Tim. *The Things They Carried.* Boston: Houghton Mifflin, 1990.

Pizer, Donald. "Henry behind the Lines and the Concept of Manhood in *The Red Badge of
    Courage.*" *Stephen Crane Studies* 10.1 (2001): 2–7.

Shaw, Mary Neff. "Apprehending the Mystery in Stephen Crane's 'A Mystery of Heroism.'"
    CLA Journal 39 (1995): 95–103.

Wertheim, Stanley, and Paul Sorrentino, eds. *The Correspondence of Stephen Crane.* 2 vols.
    New York: Columbia UP, 1988.

Zhu, Weihong Julia. "The Absurdity of Henry's Courage." *Stephen Crane Studies* 10.2 (2001):
    2–11.

PERRY LENTZ

Private Fleming's "Well-Meaning Cow": The Implications of Crane's Literary Style

Until this midafternoon moment of Private Henry Fleming's "ecstasy of self-satisfaction" (*RBC* 64), Crane's novel, with one signal exception, is remarkably faithful, in both general and specific detail, to the historical facts of the battle of Chancellorsville as they can best be understood. He shows men fighting as the weaponry of the Civil War dictated they must. He shows both the terrain in the Wilderness of Spotsylvania in northern Virginia, and the battle in which the Third Division of the Second Corps of the Army of the Potomac was immersed on the afternoon of May 2, 1863.

Even the one signal exception—the rout of a full federal brigade on an afternoon of "desultory" or "perfunctory" combat—shows not so much Crane's indifference to the historical record but, rather, his reliance upon the most significant documents available to him, the relevant reports in the *Official Records of the War of Rebellion*. A close look at the novel reveals how Crane works to reconcile what he recognized was a problematic inconsistency. Concerning those officers whose commands he had selected as the "home" of and the models for both his fictional Henderson's brigade and his fictional 304th New York Volunteer Infantry Regiment, it turns out there was a discrepancy between the official report of Major General French, on the one hand, and the official reports of his immediate superiors, subordinates, and antagonists on the other.

From *Private Fleming at Chancellorsville:* The Red Badge of Courage *and the Civil War,* pp. 93–113. Copyright © 2006 by The Curators of the University of Missouri.

109

This close assessment of the historical accuracy of Crane's novel is based, however, upon an overview that is completely absent from both the structure and the stylistic texture of the novel itself. The point of view in the novel is almost always identical to Private Fleming's own, and this is extraordinarily reinforced by the fact of Crane's impressionistic style, as we will soon see. We are entirely immersed in the world of his physical and tactile perceptions, his emotional responses, and his mental evaluations. There are no authorial intrusions to challenge the flow of Fleming's perceptions and responses, or the accuracy of his evaluations of himself. Such intrusions would elevate our perceptions above his and would interrupt our personal and immediate experiencing of his states of mind and his ways of understanding his world.

In the absence of such intrusions, Crane employs a variety of generally subtle and ironic ways of suggesting that Private Fleming may not be seeing things accurately and may not be assessing himself accurately. We saw a dramatic example in Fleming's radical revision of his personal history as he is driven toward his initiation in combat: "he had never wished to come to the war. He had not enlisted of his free will. He had been dragged by the merciless government" (*RBC* 36). We saw a subtler example in the unconscious tentativeness of Fleming's perceptions about the size of the rebel forces facing the part of the Union left-center flank held by Henderson's brigade: "he thought he could see lighter masses"; "They were suggestive of unnumbered thousands" (62). And Crane most particularly has been assuming that a reader's own knowledge of Civil War realities will be steadily fretting at the edges of the persuasiveness of Private Fleming's conceptions and evaluations. Knowledge of the actualities of Civil War battle would not deny the soldiers of the 304th their raw courage, and it would not discount what a "ghastly" and frightening thing Civil War combat was. But it surely would challenge Fleming's belief that he and his fellows are "magnificent" (64) in their first battle.

In addition to the subtle ironies in its narrative and to the closely researched accuracy of its depiction of battle, a third aspect of Crane's novel invites and directs a reader's judgment. This is his extraordinary style. Crane's portrayal of Fleming's first experience of battle is an immense literary accomplishment. Indeed perhaps it is too immense. Even sophisticated readers remember his firing-line experience this first day, May 2, 1863, whereas they forget how he experiences combat on the morning and the afternoon of May 3. This portrayal of Fleming's first experience of battle is vividly engaging and immensely persuasive, and the more so because Crane's historical sources could hardly have helped him here. You look in vain in *Battles and Leaders of the Civil War* or the *Official Records* for any verbal depiction of the actualities of Civil War combat that might have informed his presentation. Instead, the historical sources gave him a framework of verifiable details. They thus liberated his imagination to find an answerable style in which to evoke Private Fleming's experience in the imagination of a reader.

To consider exactly how that style works and, further, the kinds of judgment deeply embedded within it, we shall examine the twenty-one paragraphs in which Crane presents Private Fleming's baptism of fire. This examination will remove us once again from our close consideration of Fleming's experience on the afternoon of May 2, 1863, but the close assessment in this case will be literary rather than historical; and to achieve an understanding of the breakthrough Crane achieved in the style of his novel, and to understand how that style is in itself an implicit instrument for evaluating character, we will use literary rather than historical documents. The first is a paragraph from James Fenimore Cooper's *The Spy: A Tale of the Neutral Ground*. This romance was published in 1821, early in the period in American literature that can usefully if loosely be called "the Romantic Period" or the "American Renaissance," a period that would reach its fruition in the literature of Ralph Waldo Emerson, Nathaniel Hawthorne, Henry Thoreau, Herman Melville, and Walt Whitman, and which ended with the outbreak of the Civil War. The second two-paragraph passage is from John William DeForest's *Miss Ravenel's Conversion from Secession to Loyalty*, which was published in 1867, early in the period of American realism, a literary movement that was a response to the Civil War and an implicit rejection of the idealism that had led to it. DeForest's great contemporary realists were William Dean Howells, Mark Twain, Henry James, and Edith Wharton.

These two passages are quite different, but taken together they will reveal that if Crane could find no useful models in contemporary historical texts for his evocation of battle, the literature of his nation would not serve him much better. Approaching Crane through these passages will reveal the extraordinary nature of his stylistic achievement. Comparing the three styles will define the point of this chapter, which is that Crane's style is not only famously evocative, it also profoundly and subtly directs a reader's judgment.

The passage from Cooper is one of the very few passages in which an author of canonical stature in the American Romantic period endeavored to portray field combat between formed bodies of soldiers. In Cooper's Leatherstocking romances, guerrilla warfare is the norm, that is, combat between informal bands of men in forested terrain. Guerilla warfare stresses the sudden ambush, the sharp exchange, the duel between personalities, and it constitutes altogether the perfect setting for Natty Bumppo's superhuman qualities of marksmanship, woodcraft, and rhetoric. (In these matters, these Leatherstocking romances exactly prefigure Ernest Hemingway's own fictions about war a century later.) In contrast, this particular passage from *The Spy* depicts the climactic moment in formally conducted battle between American dragoons and British infantry:

> In the meanwhile, great numbers of the English, taking advantage
> of the smoke and confusion in the field, were enabled to get in
> the rear of the body of their countrymen, which still preserved its
> order in a line parallel to the wood, but which had been obliged
> to hold its fire, from the fear of injuring friends as well as foes.
> The fugitives were directed to form a second line within the
> wood itself, and under cover of the trees. This arrangement was
> not yet completed, when Captain Lawton called to a youth, who
> commanded the other troop left with that part of the force which
> remained on the ground, and proposed charging the unbroken
> line of the British. The proposal was as promptly accepted as it
> had been made, and the troops were arrayed for the purpose. The
> eagerness of their leader prevented the preparations necessary to
> ensure success, and the horse, receiving a destructive fire as they
> advanced, were thrown into additional confusion. Both Lawton
> and his more juvenile comrade fell at this discharge. Fortunately
> for the credit of the Virginians, Major Dunwoodie re-entered the
> field at this critical instant; he saw his troops in disorder; at his
> feet lay weltering in blood George Singleton, a youth endeared
> to him by numberless virtues, and Lawton was unhorsed and
> stretched on the plain. The eye of the youthful warrior flashed
> fire. Riding between this squadron and the enemy, in a voice that
> reached the hearts of his dragoons, he recalled them to their duty.
> His presence and word acted like magic. The clamor of voices
> ceased; the line was formed promptly and with exactitude; the
> charge sounded; and, led on by their commander, the Virginians
> swept across the plain with an impetuosity that nothing could
> withstand, and the field was instantly cleared of the enemy; those
> who were not destroyed sought a shelter in the woods. Dunwoodie
> slowly withdrew from the fire of the English who were covered by
> the trees, and commenced the painful duty of collecting his dead
> and wounded.[1]

DeForest was a veteran of the Civil War. His realistic portrayal of combat is the most striking quality of his novel, and Crane had probably read it. Here the hero, Colburne, is directing his company's advance, as skirmishers, upon rebel fortifications at Port Hudson.

"Get down!" reiterated Colburne; but the man had waited too long already. Throwing up both hands he fell backward with an incoherent gurgle, pierced through the lungs by a rifle-ball. Then a little Irish soldier burst out swearing, and hastily pulled his trousers to glare at a bullet-hole through the calf of his leg, with a comical expression of mingled surprise, alarm and wrath. And so it went on: every few minutes there was an oath of rage or a shriek of pain; and each outcry marked the loss of a man. But all the while the line of skirmishers advanced.

The sickishness which troubled Colburne in the cannon-smitten forest had gone, and was succeeded by the fierce excitement of close battle, where the combatants grow angry and savage at sight of each other's faces. He was throbbing with elation and confidence, for he had cleaned off the gunners from the two pieces in his front. He felt as if he could take Port Hudson with his detachment alone. The contest was raging in a clamorous rattle of musketry on the right, where Paine's brigade, and four regiments of the Reserve Brigade, all broken into detachments by gullies, hillocks, thickets and fallen trees, were struggling to turn and force the fortifications. On his left other companies of the Tenth were slowly moving forward, deployed and firing as skirmishers. In his front the Rebel musketry gradually slackened and only now and then could he see a broad-brimmed hat show above the earthworks and hear the hoarse whistle of a Minie-ball as it passed him. The garrison on this side was clearly both few in number and disheartened. It seemed to him likely, yes even certain, that Port Hudson would be carried by storm that morning. At the same time, half mad as he was with the glorious intoxication of successful battle, he knew that it would be utter folly to push his unsupported detachment into the works, and that such a movement would probably end in slaughter or capture. Fifteen or twenty, he did not know precisely how many, of his soldiers had been hit, and the survivors were getting short of cartridges.[2]

Now let us look at those twenty-one paragraphs from Crane's novel, *The Red Badge of Courage*, in which he depicts Fleming's first direct experience of infantry combat. The passage begins with the first glimpse of the oncoming rebels and concludes with the depiction of the casualties taken by Fleming's company during the fight.

(1) Across the smoke-infested fields came a brown swarm of running men who were giving shrill yells. They came on, stooping and swinging their rifles at all angles. A flag, tilted forward, sped near the front.

(2) As he caught sight of them the youth was momentarily startled by a thought that perhaps his gun was not loaded. He stood trying to rally his faltering intellect so that he might recollect the moment when he had loaded, but he could not.

(3) A hatless general pulled his dripping horse to a stand near the colonel of the 304th. He shook his fist in the other's face. "You've got to hold 'em back!" he shouted, savagely; "you've got to hold 'em back!"

(4) In his agitation the colonel began to stammer. "A-all r-right, General, all right, by Gawd! We—we'll do our—we-we'll d-d-do—do our best, General." The general made a passionate gesture and galloped away. The colonel, perchance to relieve his feelings, began to scold like a wet parrot. The youth, turning swiftly to make sure that the rear was unmolested, saw the commander regarding his men in a highly resentful manner, as if he regretted above everything his association with them.

(5) The man at the youth's elbow was mumbling, as if to himself: "Oh, we're in for it now! oh, we're in for it now!"

(6) The captain of the company had been pacing excitedly to and fro in the rear. He coaxed in schoolmistress fashion, as to a congregation of boys with primers. His talk was an endless repetition. "Reserve your fire, boys—don't shoot till I tell you—save your fire—wait till they get close up—don't be damned fools—"

(7) Perspiration streamed down the youth's face, which was soiled like that of a weeping urchin. He frequently, with a nervous movement, wiped his eyes with his coat sleeve. His mouth was still a little ways open.

(8) He got the one glance at the foe-swarming field in front of him, and instantly ceased to debate the question of his piece being loaded. Before he was ready to begin—before he had announced to himself that he was about to fight—he threw the obedient, well-balanced rifle into position and fired a first wild shot. Directly he was working at his weapon like an automatic affair.

(9) He suddenly lost concern for himself, and forgot to look at a menacing fate. He became not a man but a member. He felt that something of which he was a part—a regiment, an army, a cause, or a country—was in a crisis. He was welded into a common

personality which was dominated by a single desire. For some moments he could not flee no more than a little finger can commit a revolution from a hand.

(10) If he had thought the regiment was about to be annihilated perhaps he could have amputated himself from it. But its noise gave him assurance. The regiment was like a firework that, once ignited, proceeds superior to circumstances until its blazing vitality fades. It wheezed and banged with a mighty power. He pictured the ground before it as strewn with the discomfited.

(11) There was a consciousness always of the presence of his comrades about him. He felt the subtle battle brotherhood more potent even than the cause for which they were fighting. It was a mysterious fraternity born of the smoke and danger of death.

(12) He was at a task. He was like a carpenter who has made many boxes, making still another box, only there was furious haste in his movements. He, in his thought, was careering off in other places, even as the carpenter who as he works whistles and thinks of his friend or his enemy, his home or a saloon. And these jolted dreams were never perfect to him afterward, but remained a mass of blurred shapes.

(13) Presently he began to feel the effects of the war atmosphere—a blistering sweat, a sensation that his eyeballs were about to crack like hot stones. A burning roar filled his ears.

(14) Following this came a red rage. He developed the acute exasperation of a pestered animal, a well-meaning cow worried by dogs. He had a mad feeling against his rifle, which could only be used against one life at a time. He wished to rush forward and strangle with his fingers. He craved a power that would enable him to make a world-sweeping gesture and brush all back. His impotency appeared to him, and made his rage into that of a driven beast.

(15) Buried in the smoke of many rifles his anger was directed not so much against the men whom he knew were rushing toward him as against the swirling battle phantoms which were choking him, stuffing their smoke robes down his parched throat. He fought frantically for respite for his senses, for air, as a babe being smothered attacks the deadly blankets.

(16) There was a blare of heated rage mingled with a certain expression of intentness on all faces. Many of the men were making low-toned noises with their mouths, and these subdued cheers, snarls, imprecations, prayers, made a wild, barbaric song

that went as an undercurrent of sound, strange and chantlike
with the resounding chords of the war march. The man at the
youth's elbow was babbling. In it there was something soft and
tender like the monologue of a babe. The tall soldier was swearing in a loud voice. From his lips came a black procession of curious oaths. Of a sudden another broke out in a querulous way like
a man who has mislaid his hat. "Well, why don't they support us?
Why don't they send supports? Do they think—"

(17) The youth in his battle sleep heard this as one who dozes
hears.

(18) There was a singular absence of heroic poses. The men
bending and surging in their haste and rage were in every impossible attitude. The steel ramrods clanked and clanged with inces-
sant din as the men pounded them furiously into the hot rifle
barrels. The flaps of the cartridge boxes were all unfastened, and
bobbed idiotically with each movement. The rifles, once loaded,
were jerked to the shoulder and fired without apparent aim into
the smoke or at one of the blurred and shifting forms which upon
the field before the regiment had been growing larger and larger
like puppets under a magician's hand.

(19) The officers, at their intervals, rearward, neglected to
stand in picturesque attitudes. They were bobbing to and fro
roaring directions and encouragements. The dimensions of their
howls were extraordinary. They expended their lungs with prodi-
gal wills. And often they nearly stood upon their heads in their
anxiety to observe the enemy on the other side of the tumbling
smoke.

(20) The lieutenant of the youth's company had encountered a
soldier who had fled screaming at the first volley of his comrades.
Behind the lines these two were acting a little isolated scene.
The man was blubbering and staring with sheeplike eyes at the
lieutenant, who had seized him by the collar and was pommeling
him. He drove him back into the ranks with many blows. The
soldier went mechanically, dully, with his animal-like eyes upon
the officer. Perhaps there was to him a divinity expressed in the
voice of the other—stern, hard, with no reflection of fear in it.
He tried to reload his gun, but his shaking hands prevented. The
lieutenant was obliged to assist him.

(21) The men dropped here and there like bundles. The captain of the youth's company had been killed in an early part of the
action. His body lay stretched out in the position of a tired man

resting, but upon his face there was an astonished and sorrowful look, as if he thought some friend had done him an ill turn. The babbling man was grazed by a shot that made the blood stream widely down his face. He clapped both hands to his head. "Oh!" he said, and ran. Another grunted suddenly as if he had been struck by a club in the stomach. He sat down and gazed rue-fully. In his eyes there was mute, indefinite reproach. Farther up the line a man, standing behind a tree, had had his knee joint splintered by a ball. Immediately he had dropped his rifle and gripped the tree with both arms. And there he remained, cling-ing desperately and crying for assistance that he might withdraw his hold upon the tree. (*RBC* 54–60)

A reader might well bring an initial assumption to these three fictions that, as they become more "modern" and less "romantic" (Cooper is writing in the tradition of the historical romance), a greater human compassion and a greater concentration upon the human cost of combat would appear. And to some extent such a change obtains, in the contrast between Cooper and DeForest. George Singleton and Lawton have been personalized for us, but their stylized portraits as casualties does not get much purchase in our minds. The nameless soldiers hit beside Colburne hardly have individualized person-alities, but the specific details provided about their wounds (the "incoherent gurgle" of the man shot "through the lungs," for example) make the pain and death of a battle line much more forcibly apparent.

So perhaps it is surprising that in Crane's, the most "modern" of the three, there is far less concern for casualties than in either of the other two. The casualties are not named. They are described in reductive figurative lan-guage or in narrative patterns that make them more ridiculous than pitiable: "The men dropped here and there like bundles"; the dead captain looks like a "tired man resting," albeit looking "astonished and sorrowful" as though "some friend had done him an ill turn." A man struck in the body "grunted suddenly as if he had been struck by a club" and gazes "ruefully"; a man with a "splintered" knee clings ludicrously to a tree. They are rendered solely in terms of visual impressions; the humanity implicit in the Irish soldier's "comical" mixture of emotions in DeForest's account is denied them.

Each passage uses the third-person point of view. But in each succeed-ing example, this point of view comes steadily closer to the individual. In Cooper's passage, we are not hampered by the smoke that masks the British retreat, or by the anger Dunwoodie feels but manages to channel into effec-tive action. Such emotions obviously are present in Captain Colburne, which DeForest's account specifically witnesses: fear ("sickishness") earlier, and now

"He was throbbing with elation and confidence" and "felt as if he could take Port Hudson with his detachment alone." He is, however, only "half mad" and still quite capable of exercising judicious restraint.

In Crane's narrative, on the other hand, we are blinded by the smoke, alongside Private Fleming. All Crane gives us are the emotions, in the bewildering sequence as they surge over Fleming. Colburne and Dunwoodie are experienced officers, granted, whereas Fleming is an inexperienced private soldier. But when juxtaposed to DeForest's sober and realistic account, Crane's passage appears other than "realistic," even at first glance. Compare "He developed the acute exasperation of a pestered animal, a well-meaning cow worried by dogs" (no. 14), with "He was throbbing with elation and confidence, for he had cleaned off the gunners from the two pieces in his front." Which thought pattern seems more "realistic," in the sense of being more probably true of a man in armed combat? How many infantrymen are likely to think of themselves as a "well-meaning cow"?

The focus in Crane is upon the sensory impressions of battle, which is not the case in the other two. But consider the implications of what is revealed about Private Fleming's mental condition. In *The Spy*, there is smoke and confusion and fear; indeed, the dragoons are thrown into confused disorder. Cooper's focus is not on these, however, but on the commanders' leadership; their encouragement, direction, and deployment of their men in response to clearly perceived situations. In the passage from DeForest's *Miss Ravenel's Conversion*, there is more stress on the sights, sounds, and emotions of battle, and considerable attention paid to the emotions sweeping through the hero. But again, these do not explicitly interfere either with Colburne's intelligent command of his men or with his understanding of the nature of the action in which they are engaged.

In Crane's novel, Private Fleming's emotions and sensory perceptions are stressed to the exclusion of everything else. The central paragraphs in this portion can each be catalogued according to a single sensory impression or a single emotion: in no. 7 it is perspiration, in no. 8 panicked firing, no. 9 loyalty, no. 10 the racket of their gunfire, no. 11 brotherhood, no. 12 work, no. 13 the tactile world of fleshly sensations, no. 14 rage, no. 15 smell, no. 16 voices, no. 17 numbness, no. 18 the sight of their firing line. Further, these paragraphs are arrayed without order, in deliberate incoherence: clearly no. 8 should follow no. 1 directly, but a sweep of disordered impressions intervenes, confirming that Fleming immediately loses all sense of time.

One of the first (famous) consequences in Crane's depiction is a specific repudiation of conventional glamour: here there is no eye that flashes fire. "There was a singular absence of heroic poses" (no. 18) among the men, while the officers "neglected to stand in picturesque attitudes" (no. 19). There are no heroic poses in DeForest's account, either, where solid paragraphs reflect Colburne's mind, in which "the glorious intoxication of successful battle" is controlled by wisdom and discipline, just as reference to those emotions is buried in a paragraph of sober narrative. What Colburne sees (the increasing scarcity of "broad-brimmed" hats above the rebel parapets) provides him with information from which to make decisions. Crane's style conveys just the opposite: as the narrative disintegrates into unconnected fragments and random emotions, perceptions, and impressions, so too (it is implied) does Private Fleming's mind.

This is not the case of everyone on the firing line. Lieutenant Hasbrouck, as inexperienced as Private Fleming, behaves with extraordinary intelligence. He blocks the flight of a fear-struck private, drives him back into the ranks, and despite his own wounded hand somehow manages to help him reload his gun. The point of view is so close to Fleming that a reader instinctively attributes to Fleming himself the admiring assessment of Hasbrouck's soldierly conduct: "Perhaps there was . . . a divinity expressed in" Lieutenant Hasbrouck's "voice . . .—stern, hard, with no reflection of fear in it" (no. 20). Compare the concept of "divinity" with Colburne's businesslike mein: "Fifteen or twenty, he did not know precisely how many, of his soldiers had been hit, and the survivors were getting short of cartridges."

These three passages have quite different rhetorical styles. Cooper's metaphorical range is slight and utterly conventional: "the horse" is a standard eighteenth- and nineteenth-century synecdoche for cavalry. "The eye of the youthful warrior flashed fire" is so conventional as to find no purchase in the reader's mind. So is the claim that his voice "reached the hearts of his dragoons," or that "His presence and word acted like magic."

DeForest is writing about the most cataclysmic and significant war in American history, a war he had witnessed as a serving officer, yet his style is as minimalist as any current novelist writing about bored, affluent collegians. His skirmish fire has literally, not metaphorically, "cleaned off" the rebel gunners from their artillery pieces. There is not a single example of figurative language in these two paragraphs. This is not always the case with DeForest, but generally he is determined to show things with the clarity of flat depiction, to show things as they are.

With Crane, it could almost be said he chooses figurative language in such a way as to show how things were not. The range of his figurative language and style is startling. There are unexpected, often ironic or paradoxical similes. Colonel MacChesnay begins "to scold like a wet parrot" (no. 4); the captain speaks to his company "as to a congregation of boys with primers" (no. 6); Private Fleming's face is "soiled like that of a weeping urchin" (no. 7); the regiment in action is "like a firework that, once ignited, proceeds superior to circumstances until its blazing vitality fades" (no. 10); in action on the firing line, trying to kill rebel soldiers, he is "like a carpenter who has made many boxes, making still another box" (no. 12); his eyeballs are "like hot stones" (no. 13); the babbling of one soldier in battle is "like the monologue of a babe," while a complaining soldier speaks "like a man who has mislaid his hat" (no. 16); Fleming, engaged in combat, "heard this as one who dozes hears" (no. 17); approaching rebel infantry, glimpsed through the smoke, seem to have been "growing larger and larger like puppets under a magician's hand" (no. 18).

There are likewise unexpected and often paradoxical metaphors. To his own fragmented perception, Private Fleming's "sweat" is "blistering" rather than cooling (no. 13). The appropriate "red rage" of the battle experience devolves into the bizarre metaphor of "the acute exasperation of a pestered animal, a well-meaning cow worried by dogs" (no. 14). This metaphor refers to a soldier in an army that has invaded an enemy's land, who has had a winter of training, who is armed with the most murderous weaponry his government can afford to put in his hands. His enemies seem to him to be "swirling battle phantoms," which is appropriate enough to the difficulty of seeing through the smoke; but these "phantoms" are "choking him, stuffing their smoke robes down his parched throat," and he fights against them "as a babe being smothered attacks the deadly blankets" (no. 15). It is a rifle and not a soldier that is "obedient" (no. 8); flaps of the leather cartridge boxes bob "idiotically" (no. 18). There are bizarre dual sensory appeals: "jolted dreams" (no. 12), "blistering sweat," a "burning roar" (no. 17).

Crane's style is by far the most vivid of the three. Cooper's style is so conventional we must stimulate our own imagination (which proves hard indeed) in order to envision his portrait of combat. The flatness of DeForest's style, his reliance upon narrative alone to carry us, is what we are schooled to expect by much of the literature of our day. What we are perhaps not prepared for is the hero's (and DeForest's own) unalloyed commitment to the Union cause: his flat style remains, surprisingly to our anticipation, uninflected by irony.

In contrast, Crane's style is inflated, at times overly so (he sometimes becomes his own best, or worst, parodist). It is violently stimulating to the imagination. The paradoxical imagery of "blistering sweat" and the dual sensory appeal of "burning roar" demand a vicarious response. The same is true of the extraordinary, ironic, "inappropriate," or paradoxical range of figurative language. Yoking a private soldier in the Army of the Potomac, who is firing his rifle furiously in combat, to a "well-meaning cow" presents such an anomaly it snags our attention, and the image registers in a way utterly beyond anything achieved by Cooper when his hero's eyes flash fire.

Crane's style dovetails precisely with the achievement of the structure of this passage; the style also insists upon the bizarre and utter chaos of Private Fleming's experiencing of this moment. The steady, almost leechlike attachment of the novel's point of view to Fleming's own individual perception means that we implicitly credit him with these reactions, just as we tend to credit him with seeing something akin to divinity in Hasbrouck's competent performance of his job. "He developed the acute exasperation of a pestered animal, a well-meaning cow worried by dogs" (no. 14). We assume not only that Fleming feels this "exasperation" but also that the image of the cow is his own. Instinctively we assume that this very image flashed into his own, individual, consciousness. And our assumption about this specific impression (that it is Fleming's own) is reinforced by other memories of the cows of his mother's farm, which came to him earlier (*RBC* 7, 27) at particularly significant or vivid moments.

That these figures—of a carpenter making boxes, a babe fighting against blankets, or that cow—are to be attributed to Private Fleming himself is a hard thing to "prove," but it seems to me that this is the way Crane's style works upon us. We know that Fleming does, himself, feel the "blistering sweat" (no. 13) as such, and that he does himself hear the man at his elbow babbling "like the monologue of a babe" (nos. 16 and 17), and that this is how he imagines the noise to himself. It seems consistent then that these other images cross his attention, as part of those "jolted dreams" that "were never perfect to him afterward, but remained a mass of blurred shapes" (no. 12).

This "fact" about the style—that this figurative language "belongs" uniquely to Private Fleming—is made more certain by the fact that, upon reflection, we know we are "seeing" what Fleming saw. We understand that this is distinct from what Lieutenant Hasbrouck was seeing, or the way he was seeing it. Otherwise, Hasbrouck could not have performed as he did. Likewise with Fleming's fellow enlisted men: the salient difference between Fleming and Private Jim Conklin is the former's "busy mind" (*RBC* 6); Conklin, in stark contrast, is prone to violence but phlegmatic and unimaginative (16–17), given to measuring sandwiches and to the "blissful contemplation of the food he had swallowed" (43). So Conklin's reactions to his first battle were appropriately different: he "was swearing in a loud voice. From his lips came a black procession of curious oaths" (no. 16). We are surely not to believe that the extraordinary range of impressions in the passage above is at all akin to what was crossing Conklin's mind at this moment. We will have reason, also, before this night is over to believe that Fleming's experience of this afternoon's battle was vastly different from Private Wilson's experience of it.

Metaphors and similes are ways of ordering perception, of orienting ourselves in the world, of demonstrating an intellectual and human control over experience. When they are thus wildly inappropriate, we have the sense that the mind to which they are "credited" cannot orient itself. This dovetails with the disconnected, disordered narrative, centered upon that stream of conflicting emotions. Our strongest sense is that Private Fleming in this action was incapable of making sense of his experience.

The reasons? His perception was obviously distorted by an inevitable surge of adrenalin and nervous energy. But it also seems he was paying the price for his stored-up nervousness: hence his panicked surrender of self-discipline to the raw sensory details of battle, especially in the "assurance" he took from the all-enveloping "noise" of its rifle fire (no. 10). His characteristic self-absorption was ratcheted up into monstrous blindness to what was really going on around him. Thus Private Fleming's consciousness is dominated by his physical senses and his crazily excited imagination; his mind cannot pull the details of his world into significant patterns; he cannot (unlike Colburne) discipline his emotions; he cannot (unlike Hasbrouck) discipline his mind; he cannot discipline himself. Some such lack of discipline surely affected to a greater or lesser degree his fellow soldiers, which in its turn explains why they took such egregious losses in this first exchange.

If the range of figurative language credited to Fleming's imagination is startling, it is not without a pattern, one that we have seen consistently and that is peculiar to this soldier. Crane consistently calls Private Fleming "the youth." The reader tends to accept this as an alternative identification for him, and the term thus loses its meaning, but it is in fact a telling identification.

Recall that as he wrestled with his fear of failing the test of combat, Fleming conceived of it in schoolroom terms, in childish terms, without revealing any full or mature awareness of what was in store for him. The potential rewards he also conceived of in exactly such terms. If successful, he would pass a test he would not have to retake. The potential penalties for failure were public scorn and humiliation. Of the real possibility of death, wounds, and the like, he had no conception. Indeed, in his furtive glance at it, death was preferable to the agony of suspense he was undergoing: it was only "some place where he would be understood" (*RBC* 44).

As the 304th New York Volunteer Infantry Regiment was enduring the last moments before the rebel assault reached their position, "the youth thought of the village street at home before the arrival of the circus parade on a day in the spring. He remembered how he had stood, a small, thrillful boy, prepared to follow the dingy lady upon the white horse, or the band in its faded chariot" (*RBC* 53). Three more sentences follow, all dedicated to his memory of awaiting the circus parade; this paragraph offers more details about a moment from Fleming's childhood than any other single paragraph in the novel. Fleming was then in an agony of nervousness, commingled with his characteristic curiosity (52), but the moment was quiet on the battle line, and the paragraph makes clear how Fleming's mind works even without the numbing stimulus of combat. A thing he awaits in anguished nervousness is reduced to a thing (the circus parade from his childhood) that produced a nervous excitement of its own; but one that was benign, happy, unthreatening, utterly different. Such a mental reaction is his unconscious way of preparing himself for the oncoming "supreme trial," by thus masking its true nature behind this sustained moment of childhood memory. This is a plausible human reaction, though the extraordinary detail of his memory is peculiar and reinforces our awareness of the childishness of his nature. Whether this mental trick was "useful" to him or not, he was clearly not facing the reality of his present circumstance while he was buried in this detailed recollection.

Notice that throughout his first experience of battle, without exception his mind characterizes things in ways that render them more benign than they are, and in ways that almost always partake of his childhood world: "a congregation of boys with primers," "a weeping urchin," "a firework," "brotherhood" and "a mysterious fraternity," "a carpenter making boxes," "a well-meaning cow," "a babe" entangled in its blankets, "the monologue of a babe," "puppets under a magician's hand," officers nearly standing "upon their heads." This is not to say that Fleming's mind is untouched by other, more appropriate consciousness, including "red rage," a wish "to rush forward and strangle" the enemy. He even experiences one moment of selfless loyalty—though he mentally shuffles through an uncertain list of what the object of that loyalty might be ("a regiment, an army, a cause, or a country"), and this particular emotion is placed so as to suggest it is occasioned by the comforting roar of the regiment's own gunfire that is submerging him.

Looked at all together, this recurrence to things of peacetime and childhood looms inordinately large and confirms a characteristic peculiar to "the youth": he is not only young, he is still a child, and this is what marks him out. He conceives his world in childish terms: battles in terms of tests to be won. The rewards he seeks and the penalties he fears are childish: public adulation, or public scorn. It is instructive to look at his parting from his fellow schoolmates, and particularly the schoolgirls (*RBC* 10). His sexuality is of the most immature kind, and this is not because more mature sexual expression was unknown in the 1860s or not deemed suitable for expression in print (as *Miss Ravenel's Conversion* readily demonstrates). He has a child's vivid visual curiosity and eagerness to "see it all" (6), "to get a view of it" (52) at whatever cost to the sensibilities of others or the possible price to himself. He has a child's unawareness of his own mortality, and he has no awareness of the reality of death. In the aftermath of the battle, in his "ecstasy of self-satisfaction" (64) and with dead fellow soldiers at his feet, he remains untouched by its reality,

unaware of the possibility that he too could be one of those "ghastly forms";
his "busy mind" is engaged solely with the curious appearances of the corpses
(61). He is equally untouched by the agony of his wounded comrades. He has
a child's general indifference toward the suffering of others, whether a hut-
mate (104), a chance comrade (105), or his own mother (9–10). He distinctly
does not have an adult's imaginative consideration of others; he has no awareness that other people actually exist, save as they play into his own desiring.
Above all else, he has that monstrous self-absorption that we identify with
childhood, a self-absorption that is utterly solipsistic.

Is it unfair to characterize Private Fleming in this stark way, on the
basis only of his behavior and his mentality during his first experience of
combat? His personality during battle is quite consistent with the personality
that has preceded it in the novel down to this afternoon of May 2 and his
"ecstasy of self-satisfaction" (*RBC* 64). Look at an even earlier moment, when
battle was only a distant prospect. Recall that Crane has chosen for the 304th
New York the simplest, easiest approach to the Chancellorsville battlefield of
any presented in the historical record, one of the reasons he chose to place
Henderson's brigade in the Second Corps. Fleming's first night in the field on
this campaign generates the following perception.

> At nightfall the column broke into regimental pieces, and the
> fragments went into the fields to camp. Tents sprang up like
> strange plants. Camp fires, like red, peculiar blossoms, dotted the
> night.
>
> The youth kept from intercourse with his companions as much
> as circumstances would allow him. In the evening he wandered a
> few paces into the gloom. From this little distance the many fires,
> with the black forms of men passing to and fro before the crimson
> rays, made weird and satanic effects.
>
> He lay down in the grass. The blades pressed tenderly against
> his cheek. The moon had been lighted and was hung in a treetop.
> The liquid stillness of the night enveloping him made him feel
> vast pity for himself. There was a caress in the soft winds; and the
> whole mood of the darkness, he thought, was one of sympathy for
> himself in his distress. (*RBC* 26–27)

In his self-absorption and self-pity, Private Fleming's childish mentality
registers the mundane experiences of this evening's bivouac as "strange
plants," "red, peculiar blossoms," and "weird and satanic." For it is in that
human world that he knows he will be tested, and in his anxiety he registers
the human world as alien. His mentality now finds human comfort in the

natural world: grass "blades" press "tenderly against his cheek," the winds "caress" him, "the whole mood of the darkness . . . was one of sympathy for himself in his distress." Most startling of all, "the moon had been lighted and was hung in a treetop." Obviously he does not literally believe this, but it does occur to his mind at some level of his consciousness, which demonstrates the extraordinary reach of his self-pity and his self-centeredness. Anyone who has ever been punished as a child will recognize this tendency to find the human world alien and the natural world comfortingly human. This is, though, a tendency of childhood; and Private Fleming of the 304th New York Volunteer Infantry Regiment seems not only still immured in a childhood world, but immured to a depth beyond that reached by most children.

Private Fleming's equally untried fellow soldiers evidently shared to some degree his panicked, undisciplined response to combat: the narrative shows as much, and it is confirmed by the disproportionate losses they suffer. But this particularly childish cast of mind seems peculiar to Fleming. It characterizes neither Lieutenant Hasbrouck nor Private Conklin, and a reader will soon learn it is not true of Private Wilson either. It is this particular soldier's peculiar mentality that lies at the heart of Crane's novel: it is a study of solipsism of an extraordinary degree. When the regiment subsequently offers him a welcome haven that evening, replete with sympathy, care, and blankets after he has taken a blow to the head, he will think of the wilderness space it occupies as a "low-arched hall," with the stars visible "through a window in the forest" (*RBC* 135).

It is the fog of Private Fleming's peculiar mentality that is under study in this novel, rather than the "fog of battle." Yet it is probably the case that many readers regard Fleming's experience on this May afternoon as typical, and that he stands as a sort of "Everysoldier," the typical infantryman for this or any other war. This is true even of readers of considerable sophistication (see Chapter 5). How could Crane's portrayal of such an extraordinary mentality produce this?

In the first place, what is extraordinary about Private Fleming is the degree of his solipsism. Self-absorption is a human tendency we all share, and it is probably only when Fleming's condition is teased out of the narrative for display that its monstrous degree becomes apparent. All of us have feared failure of some sort and have brooded in self-absorption over it. So Fleming at first glance strikes us as "one of us." In his humdrum anonymity the word "typical" seems appropriate. But I doubt that very many of his readers past the earliest ages of childhood have ever, at any level of consciousness and however fleetingly, thought that "the moon had been lighted and was hung in a treetop."

Other things conspire to make us assess Private Fleming as "one of us," and hence, "typical." His fears are familiar, as is his fear of being ridiculed for expressing those fears. He fears combat, which is legitimate for any sane mentality. What is often overlooked is the peculiar nature of his fear—at no moment does he worry about dying, or being maimed or severely wounded. He does not approach battle confident of his own abilities, and we suspect that we would not, ourselves. It is instructive to note that Colburne's very success in *Miss Ravenel's Conversion* has a quality that separates him from us. We are not at all sure we could do as well as he does in battle, and the reverse is true for Fleming. We do not contrast ourselves to him in our imagination, for we can readily conceive of being just as uncertain, and we readily enter his mentality. After all, we have all been children. The quality of his curiosity we have all shared. It is something we all remember as being indeed entrancing. But presumably most of us have developed more mature kinds of imagination, through which we develop qualities of sympathy and compassion.

The qualities of style herein—themselves generated by his extraordinary mental condition—tend to render familiar that which in our own imaginations we dread: battle. The power of Crane's vivid style makes the battle quite "envisionable" to us, so we can experience it with vicarious excitement. Anything rendered so accessible to our imagination loses its strangeness and can be seen as part of our world, which in imagination it has indeed become. As Fleming's childish mind reduces the details of combat to things we are familiar with from our own childhood and our own mundane experiences (for instance, the way our minds do "career off in other places" while we are absorbed in some repetitive routine), battle becomes not so weirdly different from ordinary life. It becomes plausible, perceptible, "typical." Since Fleming in his solipsism is indifferent to the dead of his own company and to the suffering of the wounded, what marks combat as an extraordinary kind of human activity, utterly different from anything else, is forgotten: it seems "typical." But, in fact, Private Fleming is "typical" only in the sense that Milton's Satan, possessing sins all too familiarly ours, can be seen as "typical."

What happens next to Private Fleming confirms that it is upon his monstrous self-centeredness that Crane's novel is particularly focused. We left our close consideration of him while he was enjoying an "ecstasy of self-satisfaction" because "The supreme trial had been passed." These ecstatic "moments" will not last very long, however, and a "sudden" few moments later he will be fleeing "like a proverbial chicken" (*RBC* 64–65, 68–69). Henry Fleming's panic-stricken failure is surely the most renowned fact about this novel, familiar to people who know it only through its film versions, or by reputation.

Pausing at this cliff-edge moment allows us to recognize two crucial facts about the catastrophe that is just about to befall Private Fleming. In the first place, he did "pass" his first "trial." The unaccustomed blare, smoke, haze, confusion, and proximity to death did not panic him into flight, at first, nor did some raw instinct for survival impel him to flee the first time this survival was threatened (it seems he did not even know it was threatened). To establish this helps to isolate the specific reason he ran. Elements common to most instances of military panic are surely present: a belief that the line is not being supported against superior enemy forces (*RBC* 66, 67); "nervous weakness," "exhaustion"; a fearful exaggeration of "the endurance, the skill, and the valor" of the enemy (67). A "few" of his fellows panic because of a mixture of these things, and when Fleming sees them, a blind herd instinct consumes him with the thought that "the regiment was leaving him behind" (68).

What is so striking in Fleming's case is that these debilitating thoughts are generated in him by his self-centered blindness. He is dwelling in a fictional drama of his own devising: that, as in the academic world, there will be one "supreme trial"; that, having passed this, "The red, formidable difficulties of war" will have "been vanquished"; that by passing this one trial, he will achieve some permanent personal condition, immune to future failure. So, having passed the trial, "He felt that he was a fine fellow. He saw himself even with those ideals which he had considered as far beyond him" (*RBC* 64). It never occurs to him, in his childlike self-absorption, that circumambient reality—composed of other human beings, their own plans, intentions, and agendas—might not conform to this private drama he knows will shape his own life. Nor does it occur to him that his own psychology might not work as he is confident it will.

Circumambient reality first appears in the form of Major General Lafayette McLaws and about six thousand soldiers of the Army of Northern Virginia. In his moment of "self-satisfaction," Private Fleming's solipsism has erased them from existence. So when they attack again, Fleming's initial response is revealing, hilarious, and characteristic: "Surely, he thought, this impossible thing was not about to happen. He waited as if he expected the enemy to suddenly stop, apologize, and retire bowing" (*RBC* 66).

The refusal of the world to conform to the fiction his self-absorption has produced about himself is effective cause of Private Fleming's collapse. This refusal leads to the psychological reactions that follow in most animals when their conditioned expectations are violated: "Into the youth's eyes there came a look that one can see in the orbs of a jaded horse. His neck was quivering with nervous weakness and the muscles of his arms felt numb and bloodless. His hands, too, seemed large and awkward as if he was wearing invisible mittens. And there was a great uncertainty about his knee joints" (*RBC* 67). All this is perfectly appropriate to the moment, because Fleming, in his solipsism, has been privately conditioning himself to believe in a reality that does not exist.

Nor does his own psychology work as he has conditioned himself to believe it will. Before the battle he was "resolved to remain close upon his guard lest those qualities of which he knew nothing should everlastingly disgrace him" (*RBC* 14). But his private view of the world—which, given his solipsism, is the only reality of which he is aware—has evidently been convincing him that if he passes the trial, he will enter into some new and permanent condition "even with those ideals which he had" before "considered as far beyond him" (64), so he will no longer need to be on such guard. But he has not entered into any such condition, and those "qualities" of "nervous weakness," "exhaustion," and the like—generated in his case by his failure to be even vaguely aware of elemental realities about the world around him, that is, the continuing active presence of rebel soldiers—are loosened, unmonitored, and panic him into "blind" flight (69).

Earlier, on the line of battle, his mind had churned up relatively comforting images from the world of his childhood. Now, as his self-centered reality has been shattered, his mind produces horrifying images, most of them still from the world of childhood but this time from nightmare. "To the youth" the rebel probe "was an onslaught of redoubtable dragons. He became like the man who lost his legs at the approach of the red and green monster. He waited in a sort of a horrified, listening attitude" (*RBC* 68). "On his face was all the horror of those things which he imagined"; his lieutenant was a "peculiar creature"; "noises of battle were like stones; he believed himself liable to be crushed" (69). He is being followed by "dragons" determined on eating the fleeing soldiers; "he imagined [rebel shells] to have rows of cruel teeth that grinned at him" (70).

Fleming's failure, needless to say, does nothing to make him seem any less "typical" in most readers' responses. Uncertain whether we ourselves could "pass" the "trial," we have sympathized with his fear of failure from the outset, and we sympathize with him now. Crane's brilliance in selecting and depicting the patterns of Fleming's thought while he runs draws us quite vicariously into them. Yes, "Death about to thrust" us "between the shoulder blades" would seem far more dreadful than "death about to smite" us "between the eyes" (*RBC* 69). Yes, we too would take "one meager relief" in knowing that "the initial morsels for the dragons" pursuing us would be those men fleeing behind us (70). Yes, given the experience we have shared so vividly with Fleming, artillerymen standing to their pieces would seem to be "Methodical idiots! Machine-like fools!" and the "youthful" mounted officer trying to control his horse in their midst would probably strike us too as "a man who would presently be dead" (71). So again, our ready willingness to assess ourselves in "ordinary" and unheroic ways in responding imaginatively to portraits of battle, and to sympathize with Fleming's example, makes him still seem "typical" at this juncture.

It is not "typical" at all for soldiers to desert in battle, however. This is not to say that panic is unknown on the battlefield. It has upon occasion seized entire formations and entire armies, as well as individuals, and it did so during the Civil War. Nor is it to claim that unflinching heroism is the norm. The Civil War shows many examples of even brave, "proven" soldiers giving way to raw panic. Such panic befell many of the most veteran regiments and brigades of the rebel Army of Tennessee at Chattanooga in 1863 and Nashville in 1864. But it is the entire purpose of military discipline and training to ensure that panic remains atypical. This is surely the case even with these "fresh fish" of the 304th New York Volunteer Infantry Regiment. Whatever Fleming thinks in his blind panic, only a "few fleeting forms" (*RBC* 68) deserted when he did.

Notes

1. James Fenimore Cooper, *The Spy: A Tale of the Neutral Ground*, 85–86.
2. John William DeForest, *Miss Ravenel's Conversion From Secession to Loyalty*, 286–87.

ROY MORRIS JR.

On Whose Responsibility?: The Historical and Literary Underpinnings of The Red Badge of Courage

Few American novels are as famous—or mysterious—as Stephen Crane's *The Red Badge of Courage*. From the day it was first published in October 1895, the novel has been justly praised for its vivid battle scenes, penetrating psychological insights, and sepia-tinged historical accuracy. So powerful are the novel's effects that one Civil War veteran, a Union colonel, claimed to have served with the author at the Battle of Antietam in 1862—nine years before Stephen Crane was born.[1]

How was it possible for a twenty-two-year-old New Jersey bohemian, who freely admitted that he had "never smelled even the powder from a sham battle," to have written about the Civil War with such seeming authority? The short answer is that Stephen Crane was a genius. The longer answer is that Crane, like all good historical novelists, did his homework. Far from "writing a story of the war on my own responsibility," as he told a friend, Crane based his novel on a variety of sources, both oral and written, including the accounts of Civil War veterans in his adopted hometown of Port Jervis, New York, and the firsthand experiences of his prep school history professor, a true veteran of the Battle of Antietam. In addition, Crane pored over volumes of *Battles and Leaders of the Civil* War, a collection of reminiscences by Union and Confederate veterans, as well as the fictional works of such former soldiers as John W. De Forest and Ambrose Bierce. A closer look at Crane's sources makes it

From *Memory and Myth: The Civil War in Fiction and Film from* Uncle Tom's Cabin *to* Cold Mountain, edited by David B. Sachsman, S. Kittrell Rushing, and Roy Morris Jr., pp. 137–50. Copyright © 2007 by Purdue University.

apparent that while he supplied the genius, many others supplied the "responsibility." This does not diminish in any way the author's astonishing literary achievement, but it does help to explain how Crane, in the words of Bierce, came to be "drenched with blood [although] he knows nothing of war." With apologies to William Randolph Hearst, Crane might almost have said, "You furnish the war, I'll furnish the pictures."[2]

The Red Badge of Courage made Stephen Crane famous, but he had already attained a certain notoriety within the closed world of the New York literary scene by virtue of his scandalous first novel, *Maggie: A Girl of the Streets*. In many ways, *Maggie* was even more remarkable than *The Red Badge of Courage*—Crane's self-appointed mentor, William Dean Howells, for one, always considered it a better novel. But *Maggie*, a scathing account of a young woman's descent into poverty, prostitution, and death, sold few copies, and its almost literally starving author was reduced to burning pages of the book in the fireplace of his Bowery apartment for warmth. Barely scraping by as a freelance journalist for various New York newspapers, Crane mordantly observed, "I'd sell my steps to the grave at ten cents per foot."[3]

In the winter of 1893, Crane dropped by the art studio of his friend Corwin Linson at the corner of Broadway and 30th Street. Linson supported himself by doing illustrations for magazines, and he avidly collected back issues of the leading journals of the day. ("Old magazines flew at me from bookstalls," he said in a phrase he might have borrowed from Stephen Crane.) On this March afternoon, the writer's attention was caught by a stack of *Century* magazines lying scattered on the floor. The magazine featured a popular, long-running series, *Battles and Leaders of the Civil War*. Crane had been entertaining thoughts of writing a war story of his own, "a potboiler, something that would take the boarding school element. " He picked up an issue of the magazine—and the course of American literature changed. The more Crane read of the war, the more he became fascinated by the great event. "I got interested in the thing in spite of myself," he recalled, "and I had to do it my way." He began steeping himself in the legend and lore of the Civil War.[4]

It was an opportune time to begin such research. After nearly two decades of studiously avoiding the war—one modern historian has aptly termed the immediate postwar period "the Hibernation"—aging veterans had begun writing down their experiences for posterity. From the best-selling memoirs of Generals Ulysses S. Grant and William Tecumseh Sherman to the self-published reminiscences of the humblest private in the ranks, old soldiers were assiduously recording their memories. As Daniel Aaron has observed in his groundbreaking study of Civil War literature, *The Unwritten War*: "Anyone growing up in Crane's America could hardly have remained deaf to the echoes of that event. Memoirs, biographies, regimental histories, multivolumed chronicles, pamphlets, poems, diaries poured from the presses. The land swarmed with veterans more than ready to reminisce about the most exciting years of their lives."[5]

Crane, a congenital outsider with a great distrust of authority figures, naturally gravitated to the stories of the little men. One series of articles, in particular, caught his attention. It was the seven-part installment entitled "Recollections of a Private," by Warren Lee Goss of the 2nd Massachusetts Heavy Artillery. Goss had seen a good deal of action in the Civil War, and later had written a hair-raising account of his days as a prisoner at the infamous Confederate prison camp at Andersonville, Georgia. His series for *Century*, however, was more light-hearted, dealing mostly with his early days as a green recruit. Goss recounted the common experiences of incoming soldiers everywhere: the patriotic rush to the recruiting office, the tearful farewell to family and friends, the endless drilling and marching, the nervous waiting on the eve of battle. Modern critic Stanley Wertheim has pointed out that there was "a distinct literary convention for Civil War narratives" at the time; Wertheim said Crane might have used any number of different accounts as background for *The Red Badge of Courage*. However, the testimony of Linson—and of Crane himself, who personally thanked Mrs. Olive Brett Armstrong for loaning him her bound copies of *Battles and Leaders of the Civil War*—pinpoints Goss's work as an important primary source for the novel.[6]

A closer comparison of the two works strengthens that assumption. Readers of *The Red Badge of Courage* will remember the famous opening of the book, when the untried soldiers in the 304th New York Infantry of the Union Army of the Potomac, resting in their winter camp along the Rappahannock River in northern Virginia, are aroused by rumors of an impending battle: "The cold passed reluctantly from the earth, and the retiring fogs revealed an army stretched out on the hills, resting. As the landscape changed from brown to green, the army awakened, and began to tremble with eagerness at the noise of rumors." In the second installment of "Recollections of a Private," Goss remarks similarly that "in a camp of soldiers, rumor, with her thousand tongues, is always speaking. The rank and file and under-officers of the line are not taken into the confidence of their superiors. Hence the private soldier is usually in ignorance as to his destination. What he lacks in information is usually made up in surmise and conjecture; every hint is caught at and worked out in possible and impossible combinations. He plans and fights imaginary battles." This is precisely what the young protagonist in *The Red Badge of Courage*, Henry Fleming, finds himself doing in response to the rumors. Indeed, the central issue in the book involves the interior struggle that Henry fights with himself over the question of his moral and physical courage. In chapter 1 he is pictured lying on his bunk "in a little trance of astonishment.... He tried to mathematically prove to himself that he would not run from a battle. Previously he had never felt obliged to wrestle too seriously with this question. In his life he had taken certain things for granted, never challenging his belief in ultimate success, and bothering little about means and roads. But here he was confronted with a thing of moment. It had suddenly appeared to him that perhaps in a battle he might run. He was forced to admit that as far as war was concerned he knew nothing of himself." Goss admits to having similar doubts. "It is common to the most of humanity," he notes, "that, when confronted with actual danger, men have less fear than in its contemplation.... I have found danger always less terrible to face than on the night before the battle."[7]

There are other notable similarities between the two works. Both Goss and Crane describe the new recruits bidding farewell to their former schoolmates. In Goss's account, it is the students who are fatuous—"All our schoolmates and home acquaintances 'came slobbering around camp,' as one of the boys ungraciously expressed it. We bade adieu to our friends with heavy hearts." Crane, by contrast, stresses Henry's ridiculous self-inflation: "From his home he had gone to the seminary to bid adieu [note the identical phrasing in both accounts] to many schoolmates. They had thronged about him with wonder and admiration. He had felt the gulf now between them and had swelled with calm pride. He and some of his fellows who had donned blue were quite overwhelmed with privileges for all of one afternoon, and it had been a very delicious thing. They had strutted." Both accounts feature, as well, scenes where the soldiers' mothers send them off to war with a jar of preserves (Henry's mother packs him "a cup of blackberry jam" in his bundle). It can be argued that such gifts were commonplace in rural nineteenth-century America, but it is upon such small but authentic touches that the novelist builds a plausible narrative, and that is what Crane takes from Goss's "Recollections."[8]

Other similarities in the two accounts include descriptions of the long tedium of drill, the soldiers discarding their heavy backpacks during the march to the battlefield, and their first encounter with a dead man in the field. Again, the differences are as instructive as the similarities. In Goss's account: "We came upon one of our men who had evidently died from wounds. Near one of his hands was a Testament, and on his breast lay an ambrotype picture of a group of children and another of a young woman. We searched in vain for his name." In *The Red Badge of Courage*, Henry's regiment marches past a dead Confederate skirmisher: "He lay upon his back staring at the sky. He was dressed in an awkward suit of yellowish brown. The youth could see that the soles of his shoes had been worn to the thinness of writing paper, and from a great rent in one the dead foot projected piteously. . . . The ranks opened covertly to avoid the corpse. The invulnerable dead man forced a way for himself. The youth looked keenly at the ashen face. . . . He vaguely desired to walk around and around the body and stare; the impulse of the living to try to read in dead eyes the answer to the Question." Goss's account is straightforward, matter-of-fact; one recalls Crane's complaint while reading *Century* magazine: "I wonder that some of these fellows don't tell how they *felt* in those scraps. They spout eternally of what they *did*, but they are emotionless as rocks."[9]

Crane's emphasis in his work is entirely upon how, and what, Henry is feeling at any particular time. This is particularly true in the most famous set-piece of the novel, when the youth comes upon a decaying body lying undisturbed in a cathedral-like clearing in the forest. It is, in a way, the heart of the novel, where Henry confronts his deepest fears, and Crane lavishes upon the scene all his remarkable descriptive powers:

> At length he reached a place where the high, arching boughs made a chapel. He softly pushed the green doors aside and entered. Pine needles were a gentle brown carpet. There was a religious half light. Near the threshold he stopped, horror-stricken at the sight of a thing. He was being looked at by a dead man who was seated with his back against a columnlike tree. The corpse was dressed in a uniform that once had been blue, but was now faded to a melancholy shade of green. The eyes, staring at the youth, had changed to the dull hue to be seen on the side of a dead fish. The mouth was open. Its red had changed to an appalling yellow. Over the gray skin of the face ran little ants. One was trundling some sort of bundle along the upper lip. The youth gave a shriek as he confronted the thing. . . . He remained staring into the liquid-looking eyes. The dead man and the living man exchanged a long look. Then the youth cautiously put one hand behind him and brought it against a tree. Leaning upon this he retreated, step by step, with his face still toward the thing. He feared that if he turned his back the body might spring up and stealthily pursue him. . . . He imagined some strange voice would come from the dead throat and squawk after him in horrible menaces.[10]

Like all great creative artists, Crane first gets the physical details right, then uses those details in the service of a larger emotional truth. He doesn't care so much what Henry sees as how it makes him feel and, through those feelings, act. Some critics have complained that *The Red Badge of Courage*, judged strictly as a Civil War novel, is deficient in its historical scope. The main incidents in the book, says Daniel Aaron, "might have occurred at Sevastopol or Sedan. . . . Negroes and Lincoln and hospitals and prisons are not to be found in Crane's theater; these and other matters were irrelevant to his main concern—the nature of war and what happens to people who engage in it. . . . The war served only as his setting for an antiwar tour de force in which deluded people misread the laws of the universe and were overwhelmed." Crane would have shrugged off the first part of Aaron's criticism, but one imagines he would have agreed completely with the last. As he said himself about his earlier novel, *Maggie: A Girl of the Streets*, his overriding intent was to demonstrate that "environment is a tremendous thing in the world and frequently shapes lives." Still, he devoted a great deal of care toward getting the physical details of that environment right, whether it was a Civil War battlefield or a New York slum.[11]

Goss was not the only old soldier whose wartime memories Crane mined for his book. As a boy living for a time in Port Jervis, New York, he had listened avidly to the stories told by veterans sitting around the Orange County court house. Most of these men, as historian Charles LaRocca observes, had served in the 124th New York Volunteers, nicknamed the "Orange Blossoms." The regiment's first battle, a literal baptism of fire, was at Chancellorsville, Virginia, in May 1863. There, much like Crane's 304th New York, the regiment had marched, countermarched, and fought a desperate rearguard action near the Plank Road on the battlefield following the rout of the all-German XI Corps by Lt. Gen. Stonewall Jackson's Confederates. (Significantly, Henry encounters a terror-stricken German babbling, "Where de plank road," during his own panicky peregrinations.) Towards the end of the battle, the 124th New York had made a daring bayonet charge, breaking the enemy line and capturing a number of Rebel prisoners, another event paralleled in the novel. There was even a real-life Jim Conklin, Henry's doomed best friend, in the 124th New York, although unlike his fictional counterpart, James Conklin survived the war and returned to Orange County. It is tempting, but ultimately unknowable, to think that he might have been one of the old soldiers to whom young Stephen Crane listened.[12]

If there was any doubt that Chancellorsville was the battle depicted in *The Red Badge of Courage*, it was answered by the most authoritative source— the novelist himself—in a later short story, "The Veteran." In the story, an aged Henry Fleming recounts his wartime experiences for a group of listeners sitting on soap boxes in a country store. "Mr. Fleming," says one of the listeners, "you never was frightened much in them battles was you?" "Well I guess I was," Henry answers. "Pretty well scared, sometimes. Why, in my first battle I thought the sky was falling down. I thought the world was coming to an end. You bet I was scared. . . . The trouble was, I thought they were all shooting at me. Yes, sir, I thought every man in the other army was aiming at me in particular, and only me. It seemed so darned unreasonable, you know. I wanted to explain to 'em what an almighty good fellow I was, because I thought then they might quit all trying to hit me. But I couldn't explain, and they kept on being unreasonable—blim! blam! bang! So I run. . . . That was at Chancellorsville."[13]

Another firsthand source for *The Red Badge of Courage* was Crane's history teacher at Claverack College in upstate New York. Despite its name, Claverack College was actually a quasi-military academy, and Crane spent two years there—"the happiest period of my life," he later said—preparing for the entrance exam to the United States Military Academy at West Point. (He never took the test; his older brother William convinced him that there was no future for him in the military, since there would not be another war in his lifetime. William, of course, was wrong.) At Claverack, Crane wore the Civil War–era uniform required by the school and drilled with old muskets and bayonets salvaged from the war. He rose to the rank of cadet captain, and once berated an unfortunate underclassman who dropped his gun for being an "idiot" and an "imbecile." He displayed, said the victim of the parade-ground abuse, "a perfectly hen-like attitude toward the rank and file."[14]

Under Crane's hard-driving leadership, his company won the school's coveted Washington's Birthday award for close-order drill. One of the judges was the school's history teacher and resident Civil War hero, Brevet Brigadier General John Bullock Van Petten. "General Reverend" Van Petten, like Crane's own father, was an ordained Methodist minister. Besides teaching history and elocution, Van Petten presided over one of the tables in the school dining hall, where, one of his former students recalled, "he often recounted some of his war experiences [and] became much excited as he lived over the old days." It is not known whether Crane was one of Van Petten's lunchroom charges, but as one scholar has conjectured: "It seems certain that . . . Van Petten, who had real war anecdotes to tell, was exactly the sort of man to whom Crane would have been responsive. Under these circumstances . . . Crane would surely have disregarded no opportunity to absorb further the lore of the battlefield from this veteran whose eyes had witnessed the scenes he so eloquently described."[15]

As chaplain of the 34th New York Infantry and lieutenant colonel of the 160th New York Infantry, Van Petten had seen action in a number of Civil War battles, including such hard-fought scrapes as Williamsburg, Fair Oaks, Malvern Hill, Second Manassas, Antietam, Port Hudson, and Winchester. Crane scholar Lyndon Upson Pratt has argued that Van Petten's experience at Antietam, the bloodiest single day of the Civil War, directly influenced *The*

Red Badge of Courage. According to Pratt, Van Petten personally witnessed the rout of the 34th New York in the East Woods around Dunker Church at Antietam, including the death of the regimental color-sergeant and the rescue of the unit's flag by a young corporal (a similar episode near the end of *The Red Badge of Courage* marks Henry Fleming's transformation from coward to hero). Two years later, at the Battle of Winchester, Van Petten witnessed the rout of another Union regiment—this time not his own—and suffered a career-ending bullet wound to his leg. The general's biographer, Thomas F. O'Donnell, maintains that the latter battle made a deeper impression on Van Petten and, through him, on his students. There is, of course, no way of knowing what exactly Van Petten may have told Crane, but it is easy to connect the general's real-life regiment, the 34th New York, to Henry Fleming's fictional regiment, the 304th New York. All that's needed is an extra zero.[16]

Besides transmitting his own eyewitness experiences to Crane, Van Petten may also have put him on to an important literary source for *The Red Badge of Courage*. This was Union veteran John W. De Forest's 1867 novel, *Miss Ravenel's Conversion from Secession to Loyalty*, one of the very first fictional depictions of the war. Like Van Petten, De Forest was a Union infantry officer. He was also a friend and comrade of Van Petten's, having served with the reverend general in the Port Hudson campaign of 1862 and the Shenandoah Valley campaign of 1864. In his nonfiction account of his Civil War service, *A Volunteer's Adventures*, De Forest remembers Van Petten admiringly as "an officer of distinguished gallantry," yet sufficiently one of the boys to have run "foot races in his big boots with a private, to make the soldiers laugh at the unusual buffoonery." Again the evidence is circumstantial—Crane left behind few records of his outside reading—but as O'Donnell has suggested: "De Forest and Van Petten shared many adventures which the latter undoubtedly recalled later to student audiences that included Stephen Crane. Certainly a book from De Forest's pen . . . would have been strongly recommended by the history teacher who could vouch for the authenticity of the novel. . . . If Stephen Crane had never heard of De Forest, nor of *Miss Ravenel's Conversion*, before he came to Claverack in 1888, we may be certain that he heard of the man there, and that the novel was recommended to him by his history teacher, 'The Reverend General' John B. Van Petten."[17]

Perhaps inevitably given the period in which it was written, *Miss Ravenel's Conversion* is an odd mixture of traditional romance and hard-edged realism. The central focus of the book is an old-fashioned love triangle between a virtuous young woman, an honorable and adoring gentleman, and a dashing and colorful rogue. The lead characters are little more than stock figures: flighty heroine, solemn swain, caddish cavalier, avuncular father, interfering aunt. It is doubtful that the preternaturally modern Crane paid much attention to the book's main plot. What would have attracted his interest were the (comparatively few) scenes of Civil War combat that De Forest the veteran sprinkled through his narrative. Given his own novel's emphasis on cowardice and heroism, Crane would have been particularly interested in De Forest's depiction of skulking soldiers during the height of battle: "Grim faces turned in every direction with hasty stares of alarm, looking aloft and on every side, as well as to the front, for destruction. Pallid stragglers who had dropped out of the leading brigade drifted by ... dodging from trunk to trunk in an instinctive search for cover. . . . One abject hound ... came by with a ghastly backward glare of horror, his face colorless, his eyes projecting, and his chin shaking. Colburne cursed him for a poltroon, struck him with the flat of his sabre, and dragged him into the ranks of his own regiment. . . . Further on, six men were standing in single file behind a large beech, holding each other by the shoulders." Compare this to a similar passage in *The Red Badge of Courage*: "The lieutenant of the youth's company had encountered a soldier who had fled screaming at the first volley. . . . The man was blubbering and staring with sheeplike eyes at the lieutenant, who had seized him by the collar and was pommeling him. He drove him back into the ranks with many blows. . . . Farther up the line a man, standing behind a tree, had had his knee joint splintered by a ball. Immediately he had dropped his rifle and gripped the tree with both arms. And there he remained, clinging desperately and crying for assistance that he might withdraw his hold upon the tree."[18]

There are other similarities between the two books. In one passage in *Miss Ravenel's Conversion*, the hero, Captain Colburne, relates a curious episode:

> I had just finished breakfast, and was lying on my back smoking. A bullet whistled so unusually low as to attract my attention and struck with a loud smash in a tree about twenty feet from me. Between me and the tree a soldier, with his great coat rolled under his head for a pillow, lay on his back reading a newspaper which he held in both hands. I remember smiling to myself to see this man start as the bullet passed. . . . The man who was reading remained perfectly still, his eyes fixed on the paper with a steadiness which I thought curious, considering the bustle around him. Presently I noticed that there were a few drops of blood on his neck, and that his face was paling. Calling to the card-players, who had resumed their game, I said, "See to that man with the paper." They went to him, spoke to him, touched him, and found him perfectly dead. The ball had struck him under the chin, traversed the neck, and cut the spinal column where it joins the brain, making a fearful hole

through which the blood had already soaked his great-coat. It was the man's head, and not the tree, which had been struck with such a report. There he lay, still holding the New York Independent with his eyes fixed on a sermon by Henry Ward Beecher.[19]

In *The Red Badge of Courage*, Henry Fleming encounters a similar sight: "The captain of the youth's company had been killed in an early part of the action. His body lay stretched out in the position of a tired man resting, but upon his face there was an astonished and sorrowful look, as if he thought some friend had done him an ill turn." Such macabre sights were common on the battlefield, and Warren Lee Goss, in "Recollections of a Private," recounts yet another: "Advancing through the tangled mass of logs and stumps, I saw one of our men aiming over the branch of a fallen tree. . . . I called to him, but he did not turn or move. Advancing nearer, I put my hand on his shoulder, looked in his face, and started back. He was dead!—shot through the brain; and so suddenly had the end come that his rigid hand grasped his musket, and he still preserved the attitude of watchfulness—literally occupying his post after death."[20]

De Forest may even foreshadow Henry Fleming's famous wound, his ironic "red badge of courage," in another passage of his novel. Here, Captain Colburne witnesses another battlefield injury. "I had scarcely recovered myself when I saw a broad flow of blood stream down the face of a color-corporal who stood within arm's-length of me. I thought he was surely a dead man; but it was only one of the wonderful escapes of battle. The bullet had skirted his cap where the forepiece joins the cloth, forcing the edge of the leather through the skin, and making a clean cut to the bone from temple to temple. He went to the rear blinded and with a smart headache, but not seriously injured." Similarly, when Henry is wounded—actually, he is bashed on the head by another fear-crazed Union soldier—a friendly comrade checks his injury: "'Now Henry,' he said, 'let's have a look at yer ol' head.' The youth sat down obediently and the corporal, laying aside his rifle, began to fumble in the bushy hair of his comrade. . . . He drew back his lips and whistled through his teeth when his fingers came in contact with the splashed blood and the rare wound. 'Ah, here we are!' he said. . . . 'Jest as I thought. . . . Yeh've been grazed by a ball. It's raised a queer lump jest as if some feller had lammed yeh on th' head with a club. It stopped a-bleedin' long time ago. Th' most about it is that in th' mornin' yeh'll feel that a number ten hat wouldn't fit yeh. An' your head'll be all het up and feel as dry as burnt pork.'"[21]

Whether or not such similarities prove that Crane had read De Forest remains largely in the eye of the beholder. To be certain, De Forest read Crane. He observed to New York *Times* reporter Edwin Oviatt in 1898: "You have read Stephen Crane's *Red Badge of Courage*? It seems to me a really clever book, with a good deal of really first-class work in it. His battle scenes are excellent, though I never saw a battery that could charge at full speed across a meadow. His style is short, sharp, jerky; a style that never would have been tolerated in my day."[22]

One writer whose work Crane did read—we know because Crane tells us so—is Ambrose Bierce. Like De Forest, Bierce served in the Civil War—indeed, he probably saw more hard fighting than any other writer in American history, including his celebrated disciple Ernest Hemingway. He fought at Shiloh, Stones River, Chickamauga, Chattanooga, Resaca, Pickett's Mill, and Kennesaw Mountain, where he was almost killed by a Rebel bullet to the head. After the war, Bierce was one of the first writers to transmute his fighting experiences into fiction, producing a number of tense, terse, ironic short stories focusing typically on individual soldiers trapped in an unforgiving universe. Bierce, a noted cynic and misanthrope, did not think much of Crane—"the Crane freak," he called him, adding dismissively, "I had thought that there could be only two worse writers than Stephen Crane, namely, two Stephen Cranes." Crane, for his part, went out of his way to praise Bierce's writing, particularly his celebrated short story, "An Occurrence at Owl Creek Bridge." "That story has everything," Crane told a friend. "Nothing better exists."[23]

Bierce's influence is perhaps best seen in Crane's own short stories, particularly "A Mystery of Heroism," in which a Union private heroically fetches water for his comrades under fire, only to have two young officers carelessly drop the bucket he has so courageously brought them. In *The Red Badge of Courage*, the Biercian influence is seen primarily in the cool, somewhat sarcastic distance that Crane keeps from his main character, and in the overwhelming irony of Henry's being celebrated for a "red badge of courage" that he has received while running away. It should also be noted that many of Bierce's Civil War stories concern the problem of fear, either before or during battle. In one story, "One of the Missing," the protagonist actually dies of fright, while in two other stories, "A Tough Tussle" and "One Officer, One Man," the main characters die by their own hands rather than face the terrors of combat. A fourth story, "Killed at Resaca," concerns a young officer who dies performing an act of suicidal bravery after receiving a letter from his girlfriend accusing him backhandedly of cowardice. *The Red Badge of Courage*, of course, is concerned exclusively with Henry Fleming's internal and external struggles with his own fear.[24]

Other suggested sources for Crane's novel have ranged from the ridiculous to the sublime. It has been asserted, although never proven, that Crane was influenced by a popular 1887 novel, *Corporal Si Klegg and His "Pard,"* a fictionalized account of the Civil War service of Lt. Col. Wilbur F. Hinman of the 65th Ohio Infantry. Hinman's lengthy book—the length alone would seem to argue against anyone as restless as Stephen Crane wading through it—does include some similar episodes, including the familiar patriotic rush to enlist, the rigors and boredom of camp life, a bantering conversation with a Rebel picket, and the heroic rescue of a falling flag in the heat of battle. But Hinman's account is either broadly comic or sentimentally patriotic, two traits that are notably missing from *The Red Badge of Courage*. As Crane biographer John Berryman has observed, "Few of the correspondences rehearsed by H. T. Webster [author of an article on the subject in *American Literature*] look anything but inevitable." Moreover, Webster's contention that Crane modeled his use of vernacular after Hinman's rather less convincing depiction of countrified speech fails on two counts: first, there is no evidence that Crane ever saw Hinman's book, and second, he had already mimicked vernacular speech in *Maggie: A Girl of the Streets* and various newspaper articles, several years before he began writing *The Red Badge of Courage*.[25]

A far more artistic model for Crane's novel may have been Tolstoy's nonfiction book, *Sebastopol*, concerning the Russian siege during the Crimean War. Crane had read Tolstoy first while attending Syracuse University, and had remarked then that the Russian was "the world's foremost writer." After writing *The Red Badge of Courage*, he reiterated that view, telling William Dean Howells, "Tolstoy is the writer I admire most of all." Crane scholar James B. Colvert conjectures that Howells might have given the younger novelist a copy of *Sebastopol* when Crane called on him in the spring of 1893, a meeting at which Howells supposedly told a roomful of guests, "Here is a young writer who has sprung into life fully armed." There are a number of similarities between the two books, not altogether surprising, since they both concern young men at war. To Colvert, Tolstoy's primary influence on Crane was to demonstrate that "an appropriate dramatic method is to put the observing mind into the drama of experience—to describe the world not as it might be supposed to exist as objective reality but as it appears in the observer as a mental event. . . . [T]he crucial aim of the artist, as Tolstoy and Crane saw it, is to imagine and dramatize reality as emotional transmutations of experience."[26]

Ironically, eight years before *The Red Badge of Courage* appeared, John W. De Forest had praised Tolstoy to Howells for a different reason. "Nobody but he has written the whole truth about war and battle," said De Forest. "I tried and told all I dared, and perhaps all I could. But there was one thing I did not dare tell, lest the world should infer that I was naturally a coward, and so could not know the feelings of a brave man. I actually did not dare state the extreme horror of battle, and the anguish with which the bravest soldiers struggle through it." That task was left to Stephen Crane, and it was one at which he succeeded admirably, thanks in no small part to men such as Tolstoy, De Forest, Ambrose Bierce, Warren Lee Goss, and John Bullock Van Petten, men who, unlike Crane but very much like his fictional hero Henry Fleming, "had been to touch the great death, and found that, after all, it was but the great death."[27]

NOTES

1. R. W. Stallman, *Stephen Crane: A Biography* (New York: George Braziller, 1968), p. 181. See also Sharon Carruthers, "'Old Soldiers Never Die': A Note on Col. John L. Burleigh," *Studies in the Novel* 10 (1978), pp. 158–160.

2. Quoted in Daniel Aaron, *The Unwritten War: American Writers and the Civil War* (New York: Oxford University Press, 1973), p. 211. Stephen Crane to Mrs. Olive Armstrong, April 2, 1893, in *The Portable Stephen Crane*, ed. Joseph Katz (New York: Penguin Books, 1969), p. 187. Bierce quoted in Linda H. Davis, *Badge of Courage: The Life of Stephen Crane* (Boston: Houghton Mifflin, 1998), p. 154. Joyce Milton, *The Yellow Kids: Foreign Correspondents in the Heyday of Yellow Journalism* (New York: Harper & Row, 1989), p. xii.

3. Corwin Linson, *My Stephen Crane* (Syracuse: Syracuse University Press, 1958), p. 13.

4. Linson, *My Stephen Crane*, pp. 36–37. Davis, *Badge of Courage*, p. 64.

5. Gerald F. Linderman, *Embattled Courage: The Experience of Combat in the Civil War* (New York: Free Press, 1987), p. 266. Aaron, *The Unwritten War*, p. 211.

6. Stanley Wertheim, "*The Red Badge of Courage* and Personal Narratives of the Civil War," *American Literary Realism* 6 (Winter 1973), p. 61.

7. Stephen Crane, *The Red Badge of Courage*, in *The Portable Stephen Crane*, pp. 189, 192, 197–98. Hereafter cited as *Red Badge*. Warren Lee Goss, "Recollections of a Private, II," *Century* 29 (December 2, 1884), p. 279. Goss, "Recollections of a Private, I," *Century* 29 (November 1, 1884), p. 108.

8. Goss, "Recollections of a Private, I," p. 108. *Red Badge*, p. 195.

9. Goss, "Recollections of a Private, III," *Century* 29 (March 5, 1885), p. 776. *Red Badge*, p. 212. Linson, *My Stephen Crane*, p. 37.

10. *Red Badge*, pp. 235–36.

11. Aaron, *The Unwritten War*, 211, 215. Stanley Wertheim and Paul Sorrentino, eds., *The Correspondence of Stephen Crane* (New York: Columbia University Press, 1968), p. 52.

12. Charles LaRocca, "Stephen Crane's Inspiration," *American Heritage* 42 (May–June, 1991), pp. 108–109. *Red Badge*, p. 257.

13. Stephen Crane, "The Veteran," in *The Portable Stephen Crane*, pp. 324–25. For a fuller discussion, see Harold R. Hungerford, "'That Was at Chancellorsville': The Factual Framework of *The Red Badge of Courage*," *American Literature* 34 (January 1963), pp. 520–531.

14. Wertheim and Sorrentino, *Correspondence of Stephen Crane*, p. 12. Harvey Wickham, "Stephen Crane at College," *American Mercury* 7 (March 1926), p. 294.

15. Lyndon Upson Pratt, "A Possible Source of *The Red Badge of Courage*," *American Literature* 11 (March 1939), pp. 1–10.

16. Pratt, "A Possible Source," pp. 4–5. Thomas F. O'Donnell, "John B. Van Petten: Stephen Crane's History Teacher," *American Literature* 27 (May 1955), pp. 196–202.

17. John W. De Forest, *A Volunteer's Adventures: A Union Captain's Record of the Civil War* (Baton Rouge: Louisiana State University Press, 1996), pp. 101, 182. Thomas F. O'Donnell, "De Forest, Van Petten, and Stephen Crane," *American Literature* 27 (January 1956), pp. 579–80.

18. John W. De Forest, *Miss Ravenel's Conversion from Secession to Loyalty* (New York: Penguin Books, 2000), pp. 250–51. *Red Badge*, p. 224.

19. De Forest, *Miss Ravenel's Conversion*, pp. 269–70.

20. *Red Badge*, p. 224. Goss, "Recollections of a Private, III," p. 776.

21. De Forest, *Miss Ravenel's Conversion*, pp. 251–52. *Red Badge*, pp. 264–65.

22. Edwin Oviatt, "J. W. De Forest in New Haven," New York *Times*, December 17, 1898. Reprinted in James W. Gargano, ed., *Critical Essays on John William De Forest* (Boston: G.K. Hall, 1984), p. 42.

23. For Bierce, see Roy Morris, Jr., *Ambrose Bierce: Alone in Bad Company* (New York: Crown, 1996). Ambrose Bierce, New York *Press*, July 25, 1896. Davis, *Badge of Courage*, p. 194.

24. Ambrose Bierce, *The Collected Short Stories of Ambrose Bierce* (Lincoln: University of Nebraska Press, 1970).

25. H. T. Webster, "Wilbur F. Hinman's *Corporal Si Klegg* and Stephen Crane's *The Red Badge of Courage*," *American Literature* 11 (November 1939), pp. 285–293. John Berryman, *Stephen Crane* (Cleveland: World Publishing Company, 1962), p. 79.

26. Wertheim and Sorrentino, *Correspondence of Stephen Crane*, 232. Berryman, *Stephen Crane*, pp. 54, 68. James B. Colvert, "Stephen Crane's Literary Origins and Tolstoy's *Sebastopol*," *Comparative Literature Studies* 15 (March 1978), pp. 74–75.

27. John W. De Forest, "Letter to Howells," *Harper's New Monthly Magazine* 74 (May 1887), p. 987. For Tolstoy's influence on Crane, see also J. C. Levenson, "Introduction: *The Red Badge of Courage*," in *The Works of Stephen Crane*, vol. 2, ed. Fredson Bowers (Charlottesville: University Press of Virginia, 1975), pp. xl–xlvi, liv–lxix.

Chronology

1871	Stephen Crane is born on November 1 in Newark, New Jersey. He is the youngest child of the Reverend Jonathan Towley Crane, a Methodist minister, and Mary Helen Peck Crane.
1878–1882	Reverend Crane moves his family to Port Jervis, New York, where Stephen first attends school. After the Reverend's death in 1880, Stephen's mother moves the family to Asbury Park, New Jersey.
1891	Stephen Crane attends Syracuse University, where he meets Hamlin Garland. He leaves after his first year.
1892	Crane fails at several newspaper jobs but publishes six "Sullivan County Sketches."
1893–1894	*Maggie: A Girl of the Streets* is printed privately. Crane meets W. D. Howells. He begins work on *The Red Badge of Courage*, *George's Mother*, and a collection of poems.
1895–1896	Crane travels to Mexico. The publication of *The Red Badge of Courage* and *The Black Riders* wins him instant fame. He publishes a revision of *Maggie* with *George's Mother*. En route to Cuba, meets Cora Taylor, proprietress of a house of prostitution in Florida.
1897	Crane is shipwrecked off the coast of Florida. He bases "The Open Boat" upon the incident. He travels to Greece with Cora Taylor to cover the Greco-Turkish War. Crane writes "The

Monster" and "The Bride Comes to Yellow Sky" and becomes acquainted with Joseph Conrad.

1898   *The Open Boat and Other Tales of Adventure* is published. Crane becomes a correspondent in the Spanish-American War.

1899   Crane publishes *War Is Kind*. He resides with Cora in extravagance at Brede Place in England. He suffers a massive tubercular hemorrhage.

1900   Crane dies of tuberculosis in Badenweiler, Germany on June 5. *Whilomville Stories*, *Great Battles of the World*, and *Last Words* appear posthumously. A novel, *The O'Ruddy*, is completed by Robert Barr.

Contributors

HAROLD BLOOM is Sterling Professor of the Humanities at Yale University. Educated at Cornell and Yale universities, he is the author of more than 30 books, including *Shelley's Mythmaking* (1959), *The Visionary Company* (1961), *Blake's Apocalypse* (1963), *Yeats* (1970), *The Anxiety of Influence* (1973), *A Map of Misreading* (1975), *Kabbalah and Criticism* (1975), *Agon: Toward a Theory of Revisionism* (1982), *The American Religion* (1992), *The Western Canon* (1994), *Omens of Millennium: The Gnosis of Angels, Dreams, and Resurrection* (1996), *Shakespeare: The Invention of the Human* (1998), *How to Read and Why* (2000), *Genius: A Mosaic of One Hundred Exemplary Creative Minds* (2002), *Hamlet: Poem Unlimited* (2003), *Where Shall Wisdom Be Found?* (2004), and *Jesus and Yahweh: The Names Divine* (2005). In addition, he is the author of hundreds of articles, reviews, and editorial introductions. In 1999, Professor Bloom received the American Academy of Arts and Letters' Gold Medal for Criticism. He has also received the International Prize of Catalonia, the Alfonso Reyes Prize of Mexico, and the Hans Christian Andersen Bicentennial Prize of Denmark.

HAROLD BEAVER is a retired professor from the University of Amsterdam. He is the author of a study of *Huckleberry Finn*; he is the editor of *American Critical Essays: Twentieth Century* and the editor of titles by Melville and Poe.

MARY NEFF SHAW is a professor at Louisiana State University at Shreveport. Her publications include *Flannery O'Connor: New Perspectives*.

147

PHILIP D. BEIDLER is part of the faculty at the University of Alabama. His titles include *American Wars, American Peace: Notes from a Son of the Empire* and *Late Thoughts on an Old War: The Legacy of Vietnam*.

VERNER D. MITCHELL is associate professor and graduate coordinator in the English department at the University of Memphis. He is the author of *This Waiting for Love: Helene Johnson, Poet of the Harlem Renaissance*, and he coedited the *Anthology of American Literature*, volume two.

MAX WESTBROOK was professor emeritus of English at the University of Texas. He edited *The Modern American Novel: Essays in Criticism* and other titles; his work focused on Crane, Hemingway, and western American literature.

BENJAMIN F. FISHER is a professor at the University of Mississippi. His publications include *Poe and His Times*, which he edited, and *The Gothic's Gothic*, which he wrote.

ANDREW LAWSON is part of the faculty of arts and society at Leeds Metropolitan University. Aside from writing on Crane, he has published work on Whitman and antebellum American literature.

MICHAEL SCHAEFER is a professor at the University of Central Arkansas. He is the author of *A Reader's Guide to the Short Stories of Stephen Crane*; he also published *Just What War Is: The Civil War Writings of De Forest and Bierce*, as well as other work.

PERRY LENTZ is a professor emeritus of English at Kenyon College. He is the author of historical novels about the Civil War.

ROY MORRIS JR. is the editor of *Military Heritage* magazine and the author of books on the Civil War and post–Civil War eras, including *The Long Pursuit: Abraham Lincoln's Thirty-Year Struggle with Stephen Douglas for the Heart and Soul of America* and *The Better Angel: Walt Whitman in the Civil War*.

Bibliography

Allred, Randal W. "'The Gilded Images of Memory': *The Red Badge of Courage* and 'The Veteran.'" *War, Literature, and the Arts: An International Journal of the Humanities, Special Edition: Stephen Crane in War and Peace* (1999): 100–15.

Bais, H.S.S. *Stephen Crane, Pioneer in Technique.* New Delhi, Crown Publications: distributed by Classical Publishing Company, 1988.

Benfey, Christopher. "Two Cranes, Two Henrys." *War, Literature, and the Arts: An International Journal of the Humanities, Special Edition: Stephen Crane in War and Peace* (1999): 1–10.

Bergon, Frank. *Stephen Crane's Artistry.* New York: Columbia University Press, 1975.

Boyer, Marilyn. "The Treatment of the Wound in Stephen Crane's *The Red Badge of Courage.*" *Stephen Crane Studies* 12, no. 1 (Spring 2003): 4–17.

Brown, Bill. *The Material Unconscious: American Amusement, Stephen Crane and the Economies of Play.* Cambridge, Mass.: Harvard University Press, 1996.

Cady, Edwin H. *Stephen Crane.* Boston: Twayne Publishers, 1980.

Carney, Raymond. "Crane and Eakins." *Partisan Review* 55, no. 3 (Summer 1988): 464–73.

Clendenning, John. "Visions of War and Versions of Manhood." *War, Literature, and the Arts: An International Journal of the Humanities, Special Edition: Stephen Crane in War and Peace* (1999): 23–34.

Colvert, James B. "Unreal War in *The Red Badge of Courage.*" *War, Literature, and the Arts: An International Journal of the Humanities, Special Edition: Stephen Crane in War and Peace* (1999): 35–47.

Cox, James M. "*The Red Badge of Courage*: The Purity of War." *Southern Humanities Review* 25, no. 4 (Fall 1991): 305–20.

149

Curran, John E., Jr. "'Nobody Seems to Know Where We Go': Uncertainty, History, and Irony in *The Red Badge of Courage*." *American Literary Realism* 26, no. 1 (Fall 1993): 1–12.

DeBona, Guerric. "Masculinity on the Front: John Huston's *The Red Badge of Courage* (1951) Revisited." *Cinema Journal* 42, no. 2 (Winter 2003): 57–80.

Dooley, Patrick K. *Stephen Crane: An Annotated Bibliography of Secondary Scholarship.* New York: G.K. Hall; Toronto: Maxwell Macmillan Canada; New York: Maxwell Macmillan International, 1992.

———. "'A Wound Gives Strange Dignity to Him Who Bears It': Stephen Crane's Metaphysics of Experience." *War, Literature, and the Arts: An International Journal of the Humanities, Special Edition: Stephen Crane in War and Peace* (1999): 116–27.

Dupee, F. W., ed. *The Question of Henry James, A Collection of Critical Essays.* New York, Octagon Books, 1973 [c1945].

Esteve, Mary. "'Gorgeous Neutrality': Stephen Crane's Documentary Anaesthetics." *ELH* 62, no. 3 (Fall 1995): 663–89.

Fried, Michael. *Realism, Writing, Disfiguration: On Thomas Eakins and Stephen Crane.* Chicago: University of Chicago Press, 1987.

Gibson, Donald B. *The Red Badge of Courage: Redefining the Hero.* Boston: Twayne Publishers, 1988.

González Groba, Constante. "*The Red Badge of Courage*: Henry Fleming's Battles with Readers and Literary Critics." *Revista Canaria de Estudios Ingleses* 22–23 (April–November 1991): 129–43.

Green, Melissa. "Fleming's 'Escape' in *The Red Badge of Courage*: A Jungian Analysis." *American Literary Realism* 28, no. 1 (Fall 1995): 80–91.

Guemple, Michael. "A Case for the Appleton *Red Badge of Courage*." *Resources for American Literary Study* 21, no. 1 (1995): 43–57.

Halladay, Jean R. "*Sartor Resartus* Revisited: Carlylean Echoes in Crane's *The Red Badge of Courage*." *Nineteenth-Century Prose* 16, no. 1 (Winter 1988–1989): 23–33.

Halliburton, David. *The Color of the Sky: A Study of Stephen Crane.* Cambridge [Cambridgeshire]; New York: Cambridge University Press, 1989.

Heller, Arno. *Experiments with the Novel of Maturation: Henry James and Stephen Crane.* Innsbruck: AMOE, 1976.

Johanningsmeier, Charles. "The 1894 Syndicated Newspaper Appearances of *The Red Badge of Courage*." *American Literary Realism* 40, no. 3 (Spring 2008): 226–47.

Johnson, Claudia Durst. *Understanding* The Red Badge of Courage: *A Student Casebook to Issues, Sources, and Historical Documents.* Westport, Conn.: Greenwood Press, 1998.

Lee, A. Robert. "Stephen Crane's *The Red Badge of Courage*: The Novella as Moving Box." *Gothic to Multicultural: Idioms of Imagining in American Literary Fiction.* Amsterdam, Netherlands: Rodopi, 2009.

McDermott, John J. "Symbolism and Psychological Realism in *The Red Badge of Courage.*" *Nineteenth-Century Fiction* 23 (1968): 324–31.

Mitchell, Lee Clark, ed. New *Essays on The Red Badge of Courage.* Cambridge: Cambridge University Press, 1986.

Myers, Robert M. "A Review of Popular Editions of *The Red Badge of Courage.*" *Stephen Crane Studies* 6, no. 1 (Spring 1997): 2–15.

———. "'The Subtle Battle Brotherhood': The Construction of Military Discipline in *The Red Badge of Courage.*" *War, Literature, and the Arts: An International Journal of the Humanities, Special Edition: Stephen Crane in War and Peace* (1999): 128–40.

Nagel, James. *Stephen Crane and Literary Impressionism.* University Park: Pennsylvania State University Press, 1980.

Orr, John C. "A Red Badge Signifying Nothing: Henry Fleming's Corporate Self." *War, Literature, and the Arts: An International Journal of the Humanities, Special Edition: Stephen Crane in War and Peace* (1999): 57–71.

Pizer, Donald, ed. *Critical Essays on Stephen Crane's* The Red Badge of Courage. Boston, Mass.: G.K. Hall, 1990.

Pizer, Donald. "Henry behind the Lines and the Concept of Manhood in *The Red Badge of Courage.*" *Stephen Crane Studies* 10, no. 1 (2001): 2–7.

Reynolds, Kirk M. "*The Red Badge of Courage*: Private Henry's Mind as Sole Point of View." *South Atlantic Review* 52, no. 1 (January 1987): 59–69.

Schneider, Michael. "Monomyth Structure in *The Red Badge of Courage.*" *American Literary Realism* 20, no. 1 (Fall 1987): 45–55.

Schnitzer, Deborah. *The Pictorial in Modernist Fiction from Stephen Crane to Ernest Hemingway.* Ann Arbor, Mich.: UMI Research Press, 1988.

Sorrentino, Paul, ed. *Stephen Crane Remembered.* Tuscaloosa: University of Alabama Press, 2006.

Tavernier-Courbin, Jacqueline. "Humor and Insight through Fallacy in Stephen Crane's *The Red Badge of Courage.*" *War, Literature, and the Arts: An International Journal of the Humanities, Special Edition: Stephen Crane in War and Peace* (1999): 147–59.

Urbas, Joseph. "The Emblematics of Invulnerability in *The Red Badge of Courage.*" *Q/W/E/R/T/Y* 4 (October 1994): 255–63.

Vanouse, Donald. "Catastrophe Theory and Character Transformation in *The Red Badge of Courage.*" *War, Literature, and the Arts: An International Journal of the Humanities, Special Edition: Stephen Crane in War and Peace* (1999): 82–99.

Weatherford, Richard M., ed. *Stephen Crane: The Critical Heritage.* London; New York: Routledge, 1977, 1973.

Wertheim, Stanley. *A Stephen Crane Encyclopedia*. Westport, Conn.: Greenwood Press, 1997.

Wolford, Chester L. *The Anger of Stephen Crane: Fiction and the Epic Tradition*. Lincoln: University of Nebraska Press, 1983.

Zhu, Weihong Julia. "The Absurdity of Henry's Courage." *Stephen Crane Studies* 10, no. 2 (2001): 2–11.

Acknowledgments

Harold Beaver, "Stephen Crane: The Hero as Victim." From *The Yearbook of English Studies* 12, Heroes and the Heroic Special Number (1982): 186–93. Copyright © 1982 by the Modern Humanities Research Association.

Mary Neff Shaw, "Henry Fleming's Heroics in *The Red Badge of Courage*: A Satiric Search for a 'Kinder, Gentler' Heroism." From *Studies in the Novel* 22, no. 4 (Winter 1990): 418–28. Copyright © 1990 by the University of North Texas.

Philip D. Beidler, "Stephen Crane's *The Red Badge of Courage*: Henry Fleming's Courage in Its Contexts." From *CLIO* 20, no. 3 (Spring 1991): 235–51. Published by Indiana University Press. Copyright © 1991 by Henry Kozicki.

Verner D. Mitchell, "Reading 'Race' and 'Gender' in Crane's *The Red Badge of Courage*." From *CLA Journal* 40, no. 1 (September 1996): 60–71. Copyright © 1996 by the College Language Association.

Max Westbrook, "The Progress of Henry Fleming: Stephen Crane's *The Red Badge of Courage*." From *The CEA Critic* 61, nos. 2–3 (Winter and Spring/Summer 1999): 71–82. Copyright © 1999 by the College English Association.

Benjamin F. Fisher, "*The Red Badge of Courage* under British Spotlights Again." From *War, Literature, and the Arts* 12, no. 2 (Fall–Winter 2000): 203–12. Copyright © 2000 by Benjamin F. Fisher.

Andrew Lawson, "The Red Badge of Class: Stephen Crane and the Industrial Army." From *Literature and History* 14, no. 2 (October 2005): 53–68. Copyright © 2005 by Manchester University Press.

Michael Schaefer, "'Heroes Had No Shame in Their Lives': Manhood, Heroics, and Compassion in *The Red Badge of Courage* and 'A Mystery of Heroism.'" From *War, Literature, and the Arts* 18, nos. 1–2 (2006): 104–13. Copyright © 2006 by Michael Schaefer.

Perry Lentz, "Private Fleming's 'Well-Meaning Cow': The Implications of Crane's Literary Style." Reprinted from *Private Fleming at Chancellorsville:* The Red Badge of Courage *and the Civil War.* Copyright © 2006 by the Curators of the University of Missouri. Reprinted by permission of the University of Missouri Press.

Roy Morris Jr., "On Whose Responsibility? The Historical and Literary Underpinnings of *The Red Badge of Courage*." From *Memory and Myth: The Civil War in Fiction and Film from* Uncle Tom's Cabin *to* Cold Mountain, edited by David B. Sachsman, S. Kittrell Rushing, and Roy Morris Jr. Copyright © 2007 by Purdue University. This material is used by permission of Purdue University Press.

Every effort has been made to contact the owners of copyrighted material and secure copyright permission. Articles appearing in this volume generally appear much as they did in their original publication with few or no editorial changes. In some cases, foreign language text has been removed from the original essay. Those interested in locating the original source will find the information cited above.

Index

Characters in literary works are indexed by first name (if any), followed by the name of the work in parentheses